COTTAGE PRE

Poetry Reader
VOLUME I

Burns, Tennyson, Herbert, and Shakespeare

The cover art is "Excalibur," by Daniel Maclise (1857).

© Copyright 2017, Cottage Press
cottagepress.net

Printed in the United States of America.

POETRY READER, VOLUME I

INTRODUCTION

The ancient author Horace wrote an instruction manual for poets and playwrights entitled *Ars Poetica* (*The Art of Poetry*). In it he said, "Poets wish either to profit (instruct) or to delight." All worthy literature, including poetry, will point our souls to truth, goodness, and beauty, which ultimately both delights us and instructs us in wisdom.

Authors and poets through the ages have echoed Horace's words. Popular American poet Robert Frost said, "A poem begins in delight but ends in wisdom." Percy Shelley offers one of the most beautiful and poetical expressions of this thought:

> Poetry is a fountain forever overflowing with the waters of wisdom and delight.

This series of Poetry Readers is based on Charlotte Mason's model of poetry study. She said, "Poetry takes first rank as a means of intellectual culture. Goethe tells us that we ought to see a good picture, hear good music, and read some good poetry every day."[1] Miss Mason recommended that students focus on one poet at a time, "reading his or her poems over a complete term, or even a complete year, . . . that he may have time to do what is in him towards cultivating the seeing eye, the hearing ear, the generous heart."[2]

Each Volume in the Poetry Readers series includes three or four poets, along with several selections from Shakespeare's sonnets and plays, providing more than enough poems for a full year's poetry

---

[1] Charlotte Mason, *Volume 5: Formation of Character*, (Illinois: Tyndale House, 1989), p. 224.

[2] *Ibid*, p. 224.

study. Our six year cycle of poets will introduce students to many of the most beautiful and well-known poems in the English tongue. Our aim, in the words of Charlotte Mason, is to set an "ample feast of which everyone takes according to his needs, and leaves what he has no stomach for."

HOW TO USE THE POETRY READERS

Plan to spend six to nine weeks with each of the poets in this volume, and another two or three with Shakespeare. Choose a poem for each week, and read it aloud several times over several days during that week. That is really all there is to it! See On Reading Poetry with Children at the end of this introduction to see an example of this method in action.

The vast majority of poetry reading should be unhindered by explanations and comprehension questions, but should simply allow the reader and listeners to interact with the poet. The chief aim is simply to delight in the poem.

Here are a few additional ideas for your poetry study:

1   Make poetry study part of your daily routine. If you have more than one child, gather them all together—or better yet, choose a time when they are already gathered, like a mealtime or regular read-aloud time. Then read the poem with expression and proper pauses, but with little or no commentary.

2   Try to read the poem (or a portion of it, if it is long) at least once more during the day. Ask your students to tell you something in the poem that caught their attention or gave them delight. Do not belabor this; the main point is to read and enjoy the poem.

3   Introduce the poet. For younger students, read just a portion of the short biographical sketch provided for each poet over a few weeks. Note: Most of the introductions are quoted from classic children's anthologies in the public domain.

4   Learn to read poetry properly, and teach your students to do so as well. Pause ONLY where you see punctuation marks, not necessarily at the end of each line. Commas get a short pause; end punctuation gets a longer pause. This may take some practice, as it seems so natural to pause at the end of each line.

5   Generally, there will be more than six to nine poems included for each poet. Choose the ones that you think will appeal most to your students for your main studies, and visit the others over the time period to get a fuller flavor of the poet's work.

6   If you want to incorporate some copywork, primary and elementary students could enter a stanza or two in their copybook, perhaps adding the title of the poem, and the name of the poet. Older students could add the poem to their commonplace books. For more information on copywork and commonplace books, visit the Principles & Practices page at *thereadingmother.net*.

7   Memorize one or more of the poems. Eloquent expression is nurtured in young and old alike by this time-honored practice. Beautiful language patterns are etched in the mind, which in turn inform the habitual expression of lip and pen. In addition, young children are masters of memory, so let us capitalize on that facility while it is strongest. Children WILL memorize. It is up to us to give them worthy and useful things to dwell upon.

Try to schedule a recitation before an audience periodically.

Parents, grandparents, siblings, and friends generally make an amiable and encouraging audience, as do residents of a local elder care facility. Recitation is excellent preparation for public speaking.

8 At the end of a poetry term, ask students to read/recite their favorite poem. If you keep a Book of Centuries, remember to enter the poet in the appropriate time slot. Visit *cottagepress.net* if you do not yet have a Book of Centuries.

9 Older students who have studied scansion and figures may occasionally wish to identify them in a poem. Keep this to a minimum for your family poetry studies, though. Remember the chief purpose is to delight in the poetry!

ADDITIONAL RESOURCES

Visit Poet's Corner (*theotherpages.org/poems/*) for additional selections by the poets featured in this volume.

If you wish to further your own understanding of a particular poet or poem, look for a good trustworthy guide, such as Lewis, Tolkien, Quiller-Couch, or Sayers. Though remarkable authors and poets in their own rights, they also were literary scholars, leaving a generous body of work on various poets and poems. The Great Conversation itself provides another interesting source of commentary on fellow poets and their works. If you use contemporary analyses of classic poems, do so with great caution. Be on the lookout for the tendency to superimpose the biases of one's own age onto that of another. One happy exception is Leland Ryken, who has authored an outstanding series, *Christian Guides to the Classics*.

In addition to the regular appreciation and enjoyment provided by the method of poetry study contained in this little book, read other poems with your children from a good children's anthology, such as *Favorite Poems Old and New*, edited by Helen Ferris, or *Poems Every Child Should Know*, edited by Mary Burt.

Students from elementary through high school should also pursue a study of poetry scansion and interpretation in their English Studies class. These skills are taught in Cottage Press Language Arts courses (visit *cottagepress.net*), beginning in *Fable & Song*.

High school students should also have periods of more formal poetry study assignments in addition to the Poetry Reader. This is best done in coordination with the study of Great Books by era; for example, Greek and Roman epics when you are studying ancient Greece and Rome; Old and Middle English poetry when you are studying the era of Christendom; American poetry, Romantic poetry, and Victorian poetry where they fit into your studies of more modern eras. For help with planning a Great Books program for your students, visit Cottage Press Arts & Letters (*cottagepress. net*).

ON READING POETRY WITH CHILDREN

Master teacher Q—Sir Arthur Quiller-Couch, mentor to Lewis and Tolkien and Sayers, editor of the *Oxford Book of English Verse*—in his lecture series "On Reading With Children" gives a marvelous step-by-step example of how to read a poem with a child.

> If, then, you consent with me thus far in theory, let us now drive at practice. You have (we will say) a class of thirty or forty [*ed. note:* or three or four!] in front of you. We will assume that they know a-b, ab, can at least spell out their words. You will choose a passage for them, and you will not (if you are wise) choose a passage from "Paradise Lost"...

You take the early Milton: you read out this, for instance, from "L'Allegro":

> Haste thee, Nymph, and bring with thee
> Jest and youthful Jollity,
> Quips, and Cranks, and wanton wiles,
> Nods and Becks, and wreathed Smiles
> Such as hang on Hebe's cheek,
> And love to live in dimple sleek;
> Sport that wrinkled Care derides,
> And Laughter holding both his sides.

Go on: just read it to them. They won't know who Hebe was, but you can tell them later. The metre is taking hold of them (in my experience the metre of "L'Allegro" can be relied upon to grip children) and anyway they can see 'Laughter holding both his sides': they recognise it as if they saw the picture. Go on steadily:

> Come, and trip it as ye go,
> On the light fantastick toe;
> And in thy right hand lead with thee
> The Mountain Nymph, sweet Liberty;
> And, if I give thee honour due,
> Mirth, admit me of thy crew—

Do not pause and explain what a Nymph is, or why Liberty is the 'Mountain Nymph'! Go on reading: the Prince has always to break through briers to kiss the Sleeping Beauty awake. Go on with the incantation, calling him, persuading him, that he is the Prince and she is worth it. Go on reading—

x

Mirth, admit me of thy crew,
To live with her, and live with thee,
In unreprovéd pleasures free;
To hear the lark begin his flight,
And singing startle the dull night,
From his watch-towre in the skies,
Till the dappled dawn doth rise.

At this point—still as you read without stopping to explain,
the child certainly feels that he is being led to something. He
knows the lark: but the lark's 'watch-towre'—he had never
thought of that: and 'the dappled dawn'-yes that's just it,
now he comes to think:

Then to come, in spite of sorrow,
And at my window bid good-morrow,
Through the sweet-briar or the vine
Or the twisted eglantine;
While the cock with lively din
Scatters the rear of Darkness thin;
And to the stack, or the barn door,
Stoutly struts his dames before:
Oft listening how the hounds and horn
Cheerily rouse the slumbering Morn,
From the side of some hoar hill,
Through the high wood echoing shrill:
Sometime walking, not unseen,
By hedgerow elms on hillocks green,
Right against the eastern gate,
Where the great sun begins his state,
Robed in flames and amber light,

The clouds in thousand liveries dight;
While the ploughman, near at hand,
Whistles o'er the furrow'd land,
And the milkmaid singeth blithe,
And the mower whets his sithe,
And every shepherd tells his tale
Under the hawthorn in the dale.

Don't stop (I say) to explain that Hebe was (for once) the legitimate daughter of Zeus and, as such, had the privilege to draw wine for the gods. Don't even stop, just yet, to explain who the gods were. Don't discourse on amber, otherwise ambergris; don't explain that 'gris' in this connexion doesn't mean 'grease'; don't trace it through the Arabic into Noah's Ark; don't prove its electrical properties by tearing up paper into little bits and attracting them with the mouth-piece of your pipe rubbed on your sleeve. Don't insist philologically that when every shepherd 'tells his tale' he is not relating an anecdote but simply keeping tally of his flock.

Just go on reading, as well as you can; and be sure that when the children get the thrill of it, for which you wait, they will be asking more questions, and pertinent ones, than you are able to answer. —Sir Arthur Quiller-Couch[3]

---

[3] Arthur Quiller-Couch, *On the Art of Reading*, Lecture IV "On Children's Reading" (II), Section viii.

Robert Burns

Burns was born in a clay cottage at Alloway, Scotland, in the bleak winter of 1759. His father was an excellent type of the Scotch peasant of those days,—a poor, honest, God-fearing man, who toiled from dawn till dark to wrest a living for his family from the stubborn soil. His tall figure was bent with unceasing labor; his hair was thin and gray, and in his eyes was the careworn, hunted look of a peasant driven by poverty and unpaid rents from one poor farm to another. The family often fasted of necessity, and lived in solitude to avoid the temptation of spending their hard-earned money. The children went barefoot and bareheaded in all weathers, and shared the parents' toil and their anxiety over the rents. At thirteen Bobby, the eldest, was doing a peasant's full day's labor; at sixteen he was chief laborer on his father's farm; and he describes the life as "the cheerless gloom of a hermit, and the unceasing moil of a galley slave." In 1784 the father, after a lifetime of toil, was saved from a debtor's prison by consumption and death. To rescue something from the wreck of the home, and to win a poor chance of bread for the family, the two older boys set up a claim for arrears of wages that had never been paid. With the small sum allowed them, they buried their father, took another farm, Mossgiel, in Mauchline, and began again the long struggle with poverty.

Such, in outline, is Burns's own story of his early life, taken mostly from his letters. There is another and more pleasing side to the picture, of which we have glimpses in his poems and in his Common-place Book. Here we see the boy at school; for like most Scotch peasants, the father gave his boys the best education he possibly could. We see him following the plow, not like a slave, but like a free man, crooning over an old Scotch song and making a better one to match the melody. We see him stop the plow to listen to what the wind is saying, or turn aside lest he disturb the birds at their singing and nest making. At supper we see the family about the table, happy notwithstanding their scant fare, each child with a spoon in one hand and a book in the other. We hear Betty Davidson reciting, from her great store, some heroic ballad that fired the young hearts to enthusiasm and made them forget the day's toil. And in "The Cotter's Saturday Night" we have a glimpse of Scotch peasant life that makes us almost reverence these heroic men and women, who kept their faith and their self-respect in the face of poverty, and whose hearts, under their rough exteriors, were tender and true as steel.

A most unfortunate change in Burns's life began when he left the farm, at seventeen, and went to Kirkoswald to study surveying. The town was the haunt of smugglers, rough-living, hard-drinking men; and Burns speedily found his way into those scenes of "riot and roaring dissipation" which were his bane ever afterwards. For a little while he studied diligently, but one day, while taking the altitude of the sun, he saw a pretty girl in the neighboring garden, and love put trigonometry to flight. Soon he gave up his work and wandered back to the farm and poverty again.

When Robert was twenty-two he again left home. This time he went to the little seaport town of Irvine to learn flax dressing. For on the farm the father and brothers had begun to grow flax, and it was thought well that one of them should know how to prepare it for spinning.

Here Robert got into evil company and trouble. He sinned and repented and sinned again. We find him writing to his father, "As for this world, I despair of ever making a figure in it. I am not formed for the bustle of the busy, nor the flutter of the gay. I shall never again be capable of entering into such scenes." Burns knew himself to be a man of faults. The knowledge of his own weakness, perhaps, made him kindly to others.

When twenty-seven years of age Burns first attracted literary attention, and in the same moment sprang to the first place in Scottish letters. In despair over his poverty and personal habits, he resolved to emigrate to Jamaica, and gathered together a few of his early poems, hoping to sell them for enough to pay the expenses of his journey. The result was the famous Kilmarnock edition of Burns, published in 1786, for which he was offered twenty pounds. It is said that he even bought his ticket, and on the night before the ship sailed wrote his "Farewell to Scotland," beginning, "The gloomy night is gathering fast," which he intended to be his last song on Scottish soil.

In the morning he changed his mind, led partly by some dim foreshadowing of the result of his literary adventure; for the little book took all Scotland by storm. Not only scholars and literary men, but "even plowboys and maid servants," says a contemporary, eagerly spent their hard-earned shillings for the new book. Instead of going to Jamaica, the young poet hurried to Edinburgh to arrange for another edition of his work. His journey was a constant ovation, and in the capital he was welcomed and feasted by the best of Scottish society. This inexpected triumph lasted only one winter. Burns's fondness for taverns and riotous living shocked his cultured entertainers, and when he returned to Edinburgh next winter, after a pleasure jaunt through the Highlands, he received scant attention. He left the city in anger and disappointment, and went back to the soil where he was more at home.—William J. Long, *English Literature, Its History and Its Significance for the English-Speaking World*

Another historian gives us this picture of his celebrity in Edinburgh:

All the fine ladies and gentlemen were eager to see the plowman poet. The fuss they made over him was enough to turn the head of a lesser man. But in spite of all the flattery, Burns, though pleased and glad, remained as simple as before. He moved among the grand people in their silks and velvets clad in homespun clothes "like a farmer dressed in his best to dine with the laird"[1] as easily as he had moved among his humble friends. . .—Henrietta Marshall, *English Literature for Boys and Girls*

And so,

> In the very heyday of his success in Edinburgh, Burns began to see that he should have to return to the country, don his "hodden-grey" once again, and follow the plough. So, he turned his back on the city, married a country lassie, and settled down to a small farm at Ellisland, with high hopes that here he should be happy. But poor Burns! In spite of his warm heart and love of laughter, he yielded too easily to temptation ever to be happy. The taverns and the ale-houses saw him frequently again. How then could he make Ellisland pay? In a short time he had to sell it. With his wife and children he moved into the drab little town of Dumfries. Now he was separated from all that rustic country life and picturesque, rural scenery that had been his inspiration. He turned down no more daisies in the field; the horned moon hung no longer in his window pane. Amid the dirty streets, the gossip and dissipation of a third-rate Scottish town, he was neither in harmony with himself nor with the world. And so, at the age of thirty-seven, worn out and old before his time, the greateset poet of Scotland died.—Olive Beaupré Miller, *My Book House: Halls of Fame*

Older students may be interested in what Thomas Carlyle had to say of Burns:

> Far more interesting than any of his written works as it

---

[1] Sir Walter Scott, *Life of Burns*

appears to us are his acted ones: the Life he willed and was fated to lead among his fellow-men. These Poems are but like little rhymed fragments scattered here and there in the grand unrhymed Romance of his earthly existence, and it is only when intercalated in this at their proper places that they attain their full measure of significance. And this too, alas, was but a fragment. The plan of a mighty edifice had been sketched; some columns, porticos, firm masses of building, stand completed; the rest more or less clearly indicated; with many a far stretching tendency which only studious and friendly eyes can now trace towards the purposed termination. For the work is broken off in the middle-almost in the beginning; and rises among us, beautiful and sad, at once unfinished and a ruin.—Thomas Carlyle, "Essay on Burns"

Those who have met Sir Walter Scott will like to read more of his description of Burns from his heyday in Edinburgh:

As for Burns, I may truly say, *Virigilium vidi tantum.*[2] I was a lad of fifteen in 1786-7, when he came first to Edinburgh, but had sense and feeling enough to be much interested in his poetry, and would have given the world to know him. His person was strong and robust; his manners rustic, not clownish, a sort of dignified plainness and simplicity which received part of its effect perhaps from knowledge of his extraordinary talents. I would have taken the poet, had I not known what he was, for a very sagacious country farmer of the old Scotch school — i.e. none of your modern agriculturists, who keep labourers for their drudgery,

---

[2] Virgilium vidi tantum *Thus far, I have only seen Virgil (Ovid)*

but the *douce gudeman*[3] who held his own plough. There
was a strong expression of sense and shrewdness in all his
lineaments; the eye alone, I think, indicated, the poetical
character and temperament. It was large, and of a dark
cast, and glowed (I say literally glowed) when he spoke with
feeling or interest. I never saw such another eye in a human
head, though I have seen the most distinguished men in my
time. His conversation expressed perfect self-confidence,
without the slightest presumption. Among the men who
were the most learned of their country, he expressed
himself with perfect firmness, but without the least intrusive
forwardness; and when he differed in opinion, he did not
hesitate to express it firmly, yet at the same time with
modesty.—Sir Walter Scott, *Life of Burns*

Scott later wrote of Burns in his personal journal:

Long life to thy fame and peace to thy soul, Rob Burns!
When I want to express a sentiment which I feel strongly, I
find the phrase in Shakespeare — or thee.

---

[3] douce gudeman *respectable, sober, or circumspect head of household*

ROBERT BURNS

The Ploughman's Life (1771-1779)

As I was a-wand'ring ae[4] morning in spring,
I heard a young ploughman sae sweetly to sing;
And as he was singin', thir[5] words he did say,—
There's nae life like the ploughman's in the month o' sweet May.

The lav'rock in the morning she'll rise frae her nest,
And mount i' the air wi' the dew on her breast,
And wi' the merry ploughman she'll whistle and sing,
And at night she'll return to her nest back again.

Paraphrase of the First Psalm (1781)

The man, in life wherever plac'd,
   Hath happiness in store,
Who walks not in the wicked's way,
   Nor learns their guilty lore!

Nor from the seat of scornful pride
   Casts forth his eyes abroad,
But with humility and awe
   Still walks before his God.

That man shall flourish like the trees,
   Which by the streamlets grow;
The fruitful top is spread on high,
   And firm the root below.

But he whose blossom buds in guilt
   Shall to the ground be cast,
And, like the rootless stubble, tost
   Before the sweeping blast.

For why? that God the good adore,
   Hath giv'n them peace and rest,

---

[4] ae *one*

[5] thir *these*

But hath decreed that wicked men
   Shall ne'er be truly blest.

*To A Mouse, On Turning Her Up In Her Nest With The Plough
(1785)*

Wee, sleekit, cow'rin, tim'rous beastie,
O, what a panic's in thy breastie!
Thou need na start awa sae hasty,
   Wi' bickering brattle!
I wad be laith[6] to rin an' chase thee,
   Wi' murd'ring pattle!

I'm truly sorry man's dominion,
Has broken nature's social union,
An' justifies that ill opinion,
   Which makes thee startle
At me, thy poor, earth-born companion,
   An' fellow-mortal!

I doubt na, whiles, but thou may thieve;
What then? poor beastie, thou maun[7] live!
A daimen icker in a thrave[8]
   'S a sma' request;
I'll get a blessin wi' the lave,[9]
   An' never miss't!

Thy wee bit housie, too, in ruin!
It's silly wa's the win's are strewin!
An' naething, now, to big[10] a new ane,

---

6 laith *loath*

7 maun *must*

8 daimen icker in a thrave *an occasional ear from a bundle of twenty-four ears*

9 lave *the rest*

10 big *build*

O' foggage[11] green!
An' bleak December's winds ensuin,
   Baith snell an' keen[12]!

Thou saw the fields laid bare an' waste,
An' weary winter comin fast,
An' cozie here, beneath the blast,
   Thou thought to dwell—
Till crash! the cruel coulter[13] past
   Out thro' thy cell.

That wee bit heap o' leaves an' stibble,
Has cost thee mony a weary nibble!
Now thou's turn'd out, for a' thy trouble,
   But house or hald[14],
To thole[15] the winter's sleety dribble,
   An' cranreuch[16] cauld!

But, Mousie, thou art no thy lane,[17]
In proving foresight may be vain;
The best-laid schemes o' mice an 'men
   Gang aft agley,[18]
An'lea'e us nought but grief an' pain,
   For promis'd joy!

Still thou art blest, compar'd wi' me
The present only toucheth thee:
But, Och! I backward cast my e'e.

---

[11] foggage *grass from the second crop after haying*

[12] snell an' keen *brisk and piercing*

[13] coulter *plough*

[14] hald *holding; abode*

[15] thole *to suffer; to be afflicted with*

[16] cranreuch *hoar-frost*

[17] lane *alone*

[18] Gang aft agley *go often awry*

On prospects drear!
An' forward, tho' I canna see,
    I guess an' fear!

To A Louse, On Seeing One On a Lady's Bonnet At Church (1786)

Ha! whaur ye gaun, ye crowlin ferlie?
Your impudence protects you sairly;[19]
I canna say but ye strunt rarely,
    Owre[20] gauze and lace;
Tho', faith! I fear ye dine but sparely
    On sic a place.

Ye ugly, creepin, blastit wonner,
Detested, shunn'd by saunt an' sinner,
How daur ye set your fit upon her—
    Sae fine a lady?
Gae somewhere else and seek your dinner
    On some poor body.

Swith! in some beggar's haffet squattle;[21]
There ye may creep, and sprawl, and sprattle,
Wi' ither kindred, jumping cattle,
    In shoals and nations;
Whaur horn nor bane ne'er daur[22] unsettle
    Your thick plantations.

Now haud you there, ye're out o' sight,
Below the fatt'rels[23], snug and tight;
    Na, faith ye yet! ye'll no be right,

---

[19] sairly *sorely* or *greatly*

[20] owre *over*

[21] in some beggar's haffet squattle *in some beggar's cheek lie low*

[22] horn *louse-comb (made of horn)*; bane *bone (strength)*

[23] fatt'rels *bonnet ribbons*

The verra tapmost, tow'rin height
   O' Miss' bonnet.

My sooth! right bauld ye set your nose out,
As plump an' grey as ony groset:[24]
O for some rank, mercurial rozet,[25]
   Or fell, red smeddum,[26]
I'd gie you sic a hearty dose o't,
   Wad dress your droddum.[27]

I wad na been surpris'd to spy
You on an auld wife's flainen[28] toy;
Or aiblins some bit dubbie boy,[29]
   On's wyliecoat;[30]
But Miss' fine Lunardi! fye!
   How daur ye do't?

O Jeany, dinna toss your head,
An' set your beauties a' abread!
Ye little ken[31] what cursed speed
   The blastie's makin:
Thae winks an' finger-ends, I dread,
   Are notice takin.

O wad some Power the giftie gie us[32]
To see oursels as ithers see us!
It wad frae mony a blunder free us,

---

[24] groset *gooseberry*

[25] rozet *rosin (sticky substance sometimes used to catch varmints)*

[26] fell *dreadful*; red smeddum *medicine (in this case, poison)*

[27] dress your droddum *give you a thrashing*

[28] flainen *flannel*

[29] aiblins *perhaps*; dubbie *dirty, ragged*

[30] On's wyliecoat *On his waistcoat*

[31] ken *know*

[32] O wad some Power the giftie gie us *O would some Power give us the gift*

An' foolish notion:
What airs in dress an' gait wad lea'e[33] us,
   An' ev'n devotion!

A Bard's Epitaph (1786)

Is there a whim-inspired[34] fool,
Owre[35] fast for thought, owre hot for rule,
Owre blate[36] to seek, owre proud to snool,[37]
   Let him draw near;
And owre this grassy heap sing dool,
   And drap a tear.

Is there a bard of rustic song,
Who, noteless, steals the crowds among,
That weekly this area throng,
   O, pass not by!
But, with a frater-feeling[38] strong,
   Here, heave a sigh.

Is there a man, whose judgment clear
Can others teach the course to steer,
Yet runs, himself, life's mad career,
   Wild as the wave,
Here pause—and, thro' the starting tear,
   Survey this grave.

The poor inhabitant below
Was quick to learn the wise to know,
And keenly felt the friendly glow,

---

[33] lea'e *leave*

[34] whim-inspired *whimsical, capricious*

[35] owre *over*

[36] blate *bashful*

[37] snool *snivel*

[38] frater *brotherly*

And softer flame;
But thoughtless follies laid him low,
    And stain'd his name!

Reader, attend! whether thy soul
Soars fancy's flights beyond the pole,
Or darkling grubs this earthly hole,
    In low pursuit:
Know, prudent, cautious, self-control
    Is wisdom's root.

Address To the Unco Guide[39] *(1786)*

    My Son, these maxims make a rule,
        An' lump them aye thegither;
    The *Rigid Righteous* is a fool,
        The Rigid Wise anither:
    The cleanest corn that ere was dight[40]
        May hae some pyles o' caff[41] in;
    So ne'er a fellow-creature slight
        For random fits o' daffin.[42]
                Solomon.—Eccles. ch. vii. verse 16.

O ye wha are sae guid yoursel',
    Sae pious and sae holy,
Ye've nought to do but mark and tell
    Your neibours' fauts and folly!
Whase life is like a weel-gaun[43] mill,
    Supplied wi' store o' water;

---

[39] Unco Guide *Unholy (Uncanny) Good*

[40] dight *clothed, adorned*

[41] caff *chaff*

[42] daffin *folly*

[43] weel-gaun *smoothly running*

14

The heaped happer's[44] ebbing still,
   An' still the clap plays clatter.[45]

Hear me, ye venerable core,
   As counsel for poor mortals
That frequent pass douce[46] Wisdom's door
   For glaikit[47] Folly's portals:
I, for their thoughtless, careless sakes,
   Would here propone defences-
Their donsie[48] tricks, their black mistakes,
   Their failings and mischances.

Ye see your state wi' theirs compared,
   And shudder at the niffer;
But cast a moment's fair regard,
   What maks the mighty differ;
Discount what scant occasion gave,
   That purity ye pride in;
And (what's aft mair than a' the lave),[49]
   Your better art o' hidin.

Think, when your castigated pulse
   Gies now and then a wallop!
What ragings must his veins convulse,
   That still eternal gallop!
Wi' wind and tide fair i' your tail,
   Right on ye scud your sea-way;
But in the teeth o' baith[50] to sail,
   It maks a unco lee-way.

---

[44] happer *hopper of a mill*

[45] clatter *gossip*

[46] douce *respectable, sober*

[47] glaikit *foolish, giddy*

[48] donsie *vicious*

[49] what's aft mair than a' the lave *what often more than all the rest*

[50] baith *both*

See Social Life and Glee sit down,
 All joyous and unthinking,
Till, quite transmugrified,[51] they're grown
 Debauchery and Drinking:
O would they stay to calculate
 Th' eternal consequences;
Or your more dreaded hell to state,
 Damnation of expenses!

Ye high, exalted, virtuous dames,
 Tied up in godly laces,
Before ye gie poor Frailty names,
 Suppose a change o' cases;
A dear-lov'd lad, convenience snug,
 A treach'rous inclination—
But let me whisper i' your lug,[52]
 Ye're aiblins[53] nae temptation.

Then gently scan your brother man,
 Still gentler sister woman;
Tho' they may gang a kennin wrang,[54]
 To step aside is human:
One point must still be greatly dark,—
 The moving Why they do it;
And just as lamely can ye mark,
 How far perhaps they rue it.

Who made the heart, 'tis He alone
 Decidedly can try us;
He knows each chord, its various tone,
 Each spring, its various bias:
Then at the balance let's be mute,

---

[51] transmugrified *metamorphosed, confounded*

[52] lug *ear*

[53] aiblin *perhaps*

[54] gang a kennin wrang *go a little wrong*

We never can adjust it;
What's done we partly may compute,
   But know not what's resisted.

Auld Lang Syne (1788)

Should auld acquaintance be forgot,
   And never brought to mind?
Should auld acquaintance be forgot,
   And auld lang syne!

Chorus.—For auld lang syne,[55] my dear,
   For auld lang syne.
We'll tak a cup o' kindness yet,
   For auld lang syne.

And surely ye'll be[56] your pint stowp![57]
   And surely I'll be mine!
And we'll tak a cup o'kindness yet,
   For auld lang syne.
     For auld, &c.

We twa hae run about the braes,[58]
   And pou'd the gowans[59] fine;
But we've wander'd mony a weary fit,[60]
   Sin' auld lang syne.
     For auld, &c.[61]

---

[55] auld lang syne *old long since (very long ago or days gone by)*

[56] be *buy*

[57] stowp *cup or tankard*

[58] brae *hills, hilltops*

[59] pou'd the gowans *picked the wildflowers*

[60] fit *foot*

[61] &c *et cetera (Latin for "and the rest" - referring to the refrain)*

We twa hae paidl'd in the burn,[62]
   Frae morning sun till dine;[63]
But seas between us braid[64] hae roar'd
  Sin' auld lang syne.
    For auld, &c.

And there's a hand, my trusty fere![65]
   And gie's[66] a hand o' thine!
And we'll tak a right gude-willie[67] waught,[68]
  For auld lang syne.
    For auld, &c.

Of A' The Airts The Wind Can Blaw (1788)

Of a' the airts[69] the wind can blaw,
  I dearly like the west,
For there the bonie lassie lives,
  The lassie I lo'e best:
There's wild-woods grow, and rivers row,
  And mony a hill between:
But day and night my fancys' flight
  Is ever wi' my Jean.

I see her in the dewy flowers,
  I see her sweet and fair:
I hear her in the tunefu' birds,
  I hear her charm the air:

---

[62] burn *stream*

[63] dine *dinner-time*

[64] braid *broad*

[65] fere *companion*

[66] gie's *give us*

[67] gude-willie *goodwill*

[68] waught *draft*

[69] airts *directions*

There's not a bonie flower that springs,
   By fountain, shaw,[70] or green;
There's not a bonie bird that sings,
   But minds me o' my Jean.

Farewell to the Highlands (1789)

Farewell to the Highlands, farewell to the North,
The birth-place of Valour, the country of Worth;
Wherever I wander, wherever I rove,
The hills of the Highlands for ever I love.

Chorus.—My heart's in the Highlands, my heart is not here,
My heart's in the Highlands, a-chasing the deer;
Chasing the wild-deer, and following the roe,
My heart's in the Highlands, wherever I go.

Farewell to the mountains, high-cover'd with snow,
Farewell to the straths and green vallies below;
Farewell to the forests and wild-hanging woods,
Farewell to the torrents and loud-pouring floods.
   My heart's in the Highlands, &c.

The Banks o' Doon (1791)

Ye flowery banks o' bonie[71] Doon,
   How can ye blume sae fair?
How can ye chant, ye little birds,
   And I sae fu' o care!
Thou'll break my heart, thou bonie bird,
   That sings upon the bough!
Thou minds me o' the happy days

---

[70] shaw *a small wood, a thicket, a grove*

[71] bonie (pronounced *bonnie*) *beautiful*

When my fause[72] Luve was true.
Thou'll break my heart, thou bonie bird,
 That sings beside thy mate;
For sae I sat, and sae I sang,
 And wist na[73] o' my fate.

Aft hae I rov'd by bonie Doon,
 To see the woodbine[74] twine;
And ilka bird sang o' its Luve,
 And sae did I o' mine.
Wi' lightsome heart I pu'd a rose,
 Upon its thorny tree;
But my fause Luver staw my rose,
 And left the thorn wi' me.
Wi' lightsome heart I pu'd a rose,
 Upon a morn in June;
And sae I flourished on the morn,
 And sae was pu'd or noon.[75]

A Grace Before Dinner, Extempore (1791)

O thou who kindly dost provide
 For every creature's want!
We bless Thee, God of Nature wide,
 For all Thy goodness lent:
And if it please Thee, Heavenly Guide,
 May never worse be sent;
But, whether granted, or denied,
 Lord, bless us with content. Amen!

---

[72] fause *false*

[73] wist na *knew not*

[74] woodbine *a climbing vine*

[75] so was pu'd or noon *so was plucked before noon*

ROBERT BURNS

Sweet Afton (1791)

Flow gently, sweet Afton! amang thy green braes,[76]
Flow gently, I'll sing thee a song in thy praise;
My Mary's asleep by thy murmuring stream,
Flow gently, sweet Afton, disturb not her dream.

Thou stockdove whose echo resounds thro' the glen,[77]
Ye wild whistling blackbirds in yon thorny den,
Thou green-crested lapwing thy screaming forbear,
I charge you, disturb not my slumbering Fair.

How lofty, sweet Afton, thy neighbouring hills,
Far mark'd with the courses of clear, winding rills;
There daily I wander as noon rises high,
My flocks and my Mary's sweet cot in my eye.

How pleasant thy banks and green valleys below,
Where, wild in the woodlands, the primroses blow;
There oft, as mild Ev'ning weeps over the lea,
The sweet-scented birk shades my Mary and me.

Thy crystal stream, Afton, how lovely it glides,
And winds by the cot where my Mary resides;
How wanton thy waters her snowy feet lave,[78]
As, gathering sweet flowerets, she stems[79] thy clear wave.

Flow gently, sweet Afton, amang thy green braes,
Flow gently, sweet river, the theme of my lays;
My Mary's asleep by thy murmuring stream,
Flow gently, sweet Afton, disturb not her dream.

---

[76] braes *banks*

[77] glen *a ravine or hollow with a stream flowing through it*

[78] lave *bathe*

[79] stems *stops*

ROBERT BURNS

Robert Bruce's March to Bannockburn (1793)

At Bannockburn the English lay,—
The Scots they were na far away,
But waited for the break o' day
    That glinted in the east.

But soon the sun broke through the heath
And lighted up that field of death,
When Bruce, wi' saul-inspiring[80] breath,
    His heralds thus addressed:—

Scots, wha[81] hae wi' Wallace bled,
Scots, wham[82] Bruce has aften led,
Welcome to your gory bed,[83]
    Or to Victorie!

Now's the day, and now's the hour;
See the front o' battle lour;[84]
See approach proud Edward's power—
    Chains and Slaverie!

Wha will be a traitor knave?[85]
Wha can fill a coward's grave?
Wha sae base as be a Slave?
    Let him turn and flee!

Wha, for Scotland's King and Law,
Freedom's sword will strongly draw,
Free-man stand, or Free-man fa',
    Let him on wi' me!

---

[80] saul-inspiring *soul-inspiring; courage-inspiring*

[81] wha *who*

[82] wham *whom*

[83] bed *grave*

[84] lour *threaten, crouch*

[85] knave *lad*

By Oppression's woes and pains!
By your Sons in servile chains!
We sill[86] drain our dearest veins,
   But they shall be free!

Lay the proud Usurpers low!
Tyrants fall in every foe!
Liberty's in every blow!—
   Let us Do or Die![87]

O Were My Love Yon Lilac Fair (1793)

O were my love yon Lilac fair,
  Wi' purple blossoms to the Spring,
And I, a bird to shelter there,
  When wearied on my little wing!
How I wad mourn when it was torn
  By Autumn wild, and Winter rude!
But I wad sing on wanton wing,
  When youthfu' May its bloom renew'd.

O gin[88] my love were yon red rose,
  That grows upon the castle wa';
And I myself a drap o' dew,
  Into her bonie breast to fa'!
O there, beyond expression blest,
  I'd feast on beauty a' the night;
Seal'd on her silk-saft faulds to rest,
  Till fley'd awa by Phoebus' light!

---

[86] sill *shall*

[87] die (pronounced *dee*)

[88] gin *if*

A Red, Red Rose (1794)

O my Luve's like a red, red rose,
    That's newly sprung in June:
O my Luve's like the melodie,
    That's sweetly play'd in tune.

As fair art thou, my bonie lass,
    So deep in luve am I;
And I will luve thee still, my dear,
    Till a' the seas gang[89] dry.

Till a' the seas gang dry, my dear,
    And the rocks melt wi' the sun;
And I will luve thee still, my dear,
    While the sands o' life shall run.

And fare-thee-weel, my only Luve!
    And fare-thee-weel, a while!
And I will come again, my Luve,
    Tho' 'twere ten thousand mile!

---

[89] gang *go*

ALFRED, LORD TENNYSON

lfred Tennyson was born in 1809 in the Lincolnshire village of Somersby. His father was the rector there, and had, besides Alfred, eleven other children. And here about the Rectory garden, orchard and fields, the Tennyson children played at knights and warriors. Beyond the field flowed a brook—

"That loves
To purl o'er matted cress and ribbed sand,
Or dimple in the dark of rushy coves,
Drawing into his narrow earthen urn,
  In every elbow and turn,
The filter'd tribute of the rough woodland."[1]

Of the garden and the fields and of the brook especially, Alfred kept a memory all through his long life. But at seven he was sent to live with his grandmother and go to school at Louth, about ten miles away. "How I did hate that school!" he said, long afterwards, so we may suppose the years he spent there were not altogether happy. But when he was eleven he went home again to be taught by his father, until

---

[1] Alfred, Lord Tennyson, "Ode to Memory," 1830.

he went to Cambridge.

At home, Alfred read a great deal, especially poetry. He
wrote, too, romances like Sir Walter Scott's, full of battles,
epics in the manner of Pope, plays, and blank verse. He
wrote so much that his father said, "If Alfred die, one of our
greatest poets will have gone." And besides writing poems,
Alfred, who was one of the big children, used to tell stories
to the little ones,— stories these of knights and ladies,
giants and dragons and all manner of wonderful things.
So the years passed, and one day the two boys, Charles and
Alfred, resolved to print their poems, and took them to a
bookseller in Louth. He gave them £20 for the manuscript,
but more than half was paid in books out of the shop. So the
grand beginning was made. But the little book caused no
stir in the great world. No one knew that a poet had broken
silence.—Henrietta E. Marshall, *English Literature for Boys
and Girls*

Alfred was only seventeen years of age when his first volume of
verse, *Poems by Two Brothers,* was published—to the great delight of
their mother, who had encouraged them in their poetic pursuits.

The next year Charles and Alfred went to Cambridge.
Alfred soon made many friends among the clever young
men of his day, chief among them being Arthur Hallam,
whose father was a famous historian.

At college Tennyson won the chancellor's prize for a
poem on Timbuctoo, and the following year he published a
second little volume of poems. This, though kindly received
by some great writers, made hardly more stir than the little

volume by *Two Brothers*.

Tennyson did not take a degree at Cambridge, for, owing
to his father's failing health, he was called home. He left
college, perhaps with no very keen regret, for his heart was
not in sympathy with the teaching. In his undergraduate
days he wrote some scathing lines about it. You "teach
us nothing," he said, "feeding not the heart." But he did
remember with tenderness that Cambridge had been the spot
where his first and warmest friendship had been formed.

Soon after Alfred left college, his father died very
suddenly. Although the father was now gone the Tennysons
did not need to leave their home, for the new rector did
not want the house. So life in the Rectory went quietly on;
friends came and went, the dearest friend of all, Arthur
Hallam, came often, for he loved the poet's young sister,
and one day they were to be married. It was a peaceful
happy time—

> "And all we met was fair and good,
>   And all was good that Time could bring,
>   And all the secret of the Spring,
> Moved in the chambers of the blood."

And amid this pleasant country life the poet worked on, and
presently another little book of poems appeared. Still fame
did not come, and one severe and blundering review kept
Tennyson, it is said, from publishing anything more for ten
years.

But now there fell upon him what was perhaps the darkest

sorrow of his life. Arthur Hallam, who was traveling on the Continent, died suddenly at Vienna. When the news came to Tennyson that his friend was gone—

"That in Vienna's fatal walls
God's finger touch'd him, and he slept,"

for a time joy seemed blotted out of life, and only that he might help to comfort his sister did he wish to live. . .

Time heals all things, and time healed Tennyson's grief. But there was another reason . . . for his return to peace and hope. Another love had come into his life, the love of the lady who one day was to be his wife. At first, however, it seemed a hopeless love, for in spite of his growing reputation as a poet, Tennyson was still poor, too poor to marry. And so for fourteen years he worked and waited, at times wellnigh losing hope. But at length the waiting was over and the wedding took place. Tennyson amused the guests by saying that it was the nicest wedding he had ever been at. And long afterwards with solemn thankfulness he said, speaking of his wife, "The peace of God came into my life before the altar when I wedded her."

A few months before the wedding [William] Wordsworth, [Poet Laureate of Britain], had died. One night a few months after it Tennyson dreamt that the Prince Consort came and kissed him on the cheek. "Very kind but very German," he said in his dream. Next morning a letter arrived offering him the Laureateship.

Tennyson led a peaceful, simple life. He made his home

for the most part in the Isle of Wight. Here he lived quietly, surrounded by his family, but sought after by all the great people of his day. He refused a baronetcy, but at length in 1883 accepted a peerage and became Lord Tennyson, the first baron of his name. He was the first peer to receive the title purely because of his literary work. And so with gathering honors and gathering years the poet lived and worked, a splendid old man. Then at the goodly age of eighty-four he died in the autumn of 1892.—Henrietta E. Marshall, *English Literature for Boys and Girls*

Lord Tennyson's tenure as Poet Laureate lasted forty-two years until his death in 1892.

Of interest to our young scholars: Tennyson was not happy with the way literature was "drummed thoroughly" into the students of his day, according to his son, Hallam:

> He would lament, "They use me as a lesson book at schools and they will call me 'that horrible Tennyson.'"[2]

We trust that Lord Tennyson would approve of our poetry lessons, scanning and *studying* a select few, but reading and enjoying a multitude for their own sake, and seeking what riches of wisdom and delight we find therein.

---

2 Tennyson, Hallam, *Alfred, Lord Tennyson, A Memoir By His Son*, (London: MacMillan & Company, 1905), 16.

The Lady of Shalott[3] *(1833)*

I.

On either side the river lie
Long fields of barley and of rye,
That clothe the wold and meet the sky;
And thro' the field the road runs by
To many-tower'd Camelot;
And up and down the people go,
Gazing where the lilies blow
Round an island there below,
The island of Shalott.

Willows whiten, aspens quiver,
Little breezes dusk and shiver
Thro' the wave that runs for ever
By the island in the river
Flowing down to Camelot.
Four gray walls, and four gray towers,
Overlook a space of flowers,
And the silent isle imbowers
The Lady of Shalott.

By the margin, willow-veil'd
Slide the heavy barges trail'd
By slow horses; and unhail'd
The shallop flitteth silken-sail'd
Skimming down to Camelot:
But who hath seen her wave her hand?
Or at the casement seen her stand?
Or is she known in all the land,
The Lady of Shalott?

Only reapers, reaping early
In among the bearded barley,

---

3 "The Lady of Shallot" is Tennyson's vision of 'the fair Eliane," and her unrequired love
for Sir Launcelot. The story is told in *Le Morte d'Arthur*, by Thomas Malory.

Hear a song that echoes cheerly
From the river winding clearly,
Down to tower'd Camelot:
And by the moon the reaper weary,
Piling sheaves in uplands airy,
Listening, whispers "'Tis the fairy
Lady of Shalott".

II.

There she weaves by night and day
A magic web with colours gay.
She has heard a whisper say,
A curse is on her if she stay
To look down to Camelot.
She knows not what the curse may be,
And so she weaveth steadily,
And little other care hath she,
The Lady of Shalott.

And moving thro' a mirror clear
That hangs before her all the year,
Shadows of the world appear.
There she sees the highway near
Winding down to Camelot:
There the river eddy whirls,
And there the surly village-churls,
And the red cloaks of market girls,
Pass onward from Shalott.

Sometimes a troop of damsels glad,
An abbot on an ambling pad,
Sometimes a curly shepherd-lad,
Or long-hair'd page in crimson clad,
Goes by to tower'd Camelot;
And sometimes thro' the mirror blue
The knights come riding two and two:

She hath no loyal knight and true,
The Lady of Shalott.

But in her web she still delights
To weave the mirror's magic sights,
For often thro' the silent nights
A funeral, with plumes and lights,
And music, went to Camelot:
Or when the moon was overhead,
Came two young lovers lately wed;
"I am half-sick of shadows," said
The Lady of Shalott.

III.

A bow-shot from her bower-eaves,
He rode between the barley sheaves,
The sun came dazzling thro' the leaves,
And flamed upon the brazen greaves
Of bold Sir Lancelot.
A redcross knight for ever kneel'd
To a lady in his shield,
That sparkled on the yellow field,
Beside remote Shalott.

The gemmy bridle glitter'd free,
Like to some branch of stars we see
Hung in the golden Galaxy.
The bridle bells rang merrily
As he rode down to Camelot:
And from his blazon'd baldric slung
A mighty silver bugle hung,
And as he rode his armour rung,
Beside remote Shalott.

All in the blue unclouded weather
Thick-jewell'd shone the saddle-leather,
The helmet and the helmet-feather
Burn'd like one burning flame together,

As he rode down to Camelot.
As often thro' the purple night,
Below the starry clusters bright,
Some bearded meteor, trailing light,
Moves over still Shalott.

His broad clear brow in sunlight glow'd;
On burnish'd hooves his war-horse trode;
From underneath his helmet flow'd
His coal-black curls as on he rode,
As he rode down to Camelot.
From the bank and from the river
He flashed into the crystal mirror,
"Tirra lirra," by the river
Sang Sir Lancelot.

She left the web, she left the loom;
She made three paces thro' the room,
She saw the water-lily bloom,
She saw the helmet and the plume,
She look'd down to Camelot.
Out flew the web and floated wide;
The mirror crack'd from side to side;
"The curse is come upon me," cried
The Lady of Shalott.

IV.

In the stormy east-wind straining,
The pale yellow woods were waning,
The broad stream in his banks complaining,
Heavily the low sky raining
Over tower'd Camelot;
Down she came and found a boat
Beneath a willow left afloat,
And round about the prow she wrote
The Lady of Shalott.

And down the river's dim expanse
Like some bold seer in a trance,
Seeing all his own mischance
With a glassy countenance
Did she look to Camelot.
And at the closing of the day
She loosed the chain, and down she lay;
The broad stream bore her far away,
The Lady of Shalott.

Lying, robed in snowy white
That loosely flew to left and right
The leaves upon her falling light
Thro' the noises of the night
She floated down to Camelot;
And as the boat-head wound along
The willowy hills and fields among,
They heard her singing her last song,
The Lady of Shalott.

Heard a carol, mournful, holy,
Chanted loudly, chanted lowly,
Till her blood was frozen slowly,
And her eyes were darken'd wholly,
Turn'd to tower'd Camelot;
For ere she reach'd upon the tide
The first house by the water-side,
Singing in her song she died,
The Lady of Shalott.

Under tower and balcony,
By garden-wall and gallery,
A gleaming shape she floated by,
Dead-pale between the houses high,
Silent into Camelot.
Out upon the wharfs they came,
Knight and burgher, lord and dame,

And round the prow they read her name,
The Lady of Shalott

Who is this? and what is here?
And in the lighted palace near
Died the sound of royal cheer;
And they cross'd themselves for fear,
All the knights at Camelot:
But Lancelot mused a little space;
He said, "She has a lovely face;
God in his mercy lend her grace,
The Lady of Shalott."

from Ulysses[4] *(1842)*

It little profits that an idle king,
By this still hearth, among these barren crags,
Match'd with an aged wife, I mete and dole
Unequal laws unto a savage race,
That hoard, and sleep, and feed, and know not me.

I cannot rest from travel: I will drink
Life to the lees: All times I have enjoy'd
Greatly, have suffer'd greatly, both with those
That loved me, and alone, on shore, and when
Thro' scudding drifts the rainy Hyades
Vext the dim sea: I am become a name;
For always roaming with a hungry heart
Much have I seen and known; cities of men
And manners, climates, councils, governments,

---

[4] "Ulysses" is based on Homer's *Odyssey*, of course, but also Dante's *Divine Comedy*, where Ulysses is condemned to a circle of hell well below Paris and Helen, but not very far above Judas (Canto XXVI). His crimes include fraud towards his men and towards his family. Ulysses tells Dante and Virgil how his restlessness after his return home caused him to sail beyond the western edge of the world where his ship was lost and he perished. Dante's portrayal of Ulysses was probably influenced by Virgil's Ulysses in the *Aeneid*.

Myself not least, but honour'd of them all;
And drunk delight of battle with my peers,
Far on the ringing plains of windy Troy.
I am a part of all that I have met;
Yet all experience is an arch wherethro'
Gleams that untravell'd world whose margin fades
For ever and forever when I move.
How dull it is to pause, to make an end,
To rust unburnish'd, not to shine in use!
As tho' to breathe were life! Life piled on life
Were all too little, and of one to me
Little remains: but every hour is saved
From that eternal silence, something more,
A bringer of new things; and vile it were
For some three suns to store and hoard myself,
And this gray spirit yearning in desire
To follow knowledge like a sinking star,
Beyond the utmost bound of human thought.

　　This is my son, mine own Telemachus,
To whom I leave the sceptre and the isle,—
Well-loved of me, discerning to fulfil
This labour, by slow prudence to make mild
A rugged people, and thro' soft degrees
Subdue them to the useful and the good.
Most blameless is he, centred in the sphere
Of common duties, decent not to fail
In offices of tenderness, and pay
Meet adoration to my household gods,
When I am gone. He works his work, I mine.

　　There lies the port; the vessel puffs her sail:
There gloom the dark, broad seas. My mariners,
Souls that have toil'd, and wrought, and thought with me—
That ever with a frolic welcome took
The thunder and the sunshine, and opposed

Free hearts, free foreheads—you and I are old;
Old age hath yet his honour and his toil;
Death closes all: but something ere the end,
Some work of noble note, may yet be done,
Not unbecoming men that strove with Gods.
The lights begin to twinkle from the rocks:
The long day wanes: the slow moon climbs: the deep
Moans round with many voices. Come, my friends,
'T is not too late to seek a newer world.
Push off, and sitting well in order smite
The sounding furrows; for my purpose holds
To sail beyond the sunset, and the baths
Of all the western stars, until I die.
It may be that the gulfs will wash us down:
It may be we shall touch the Happy Isles,
And see the great Achilles, whom we knew.
Tho' much is taken, much abides; and tho'
We are not now that strength which in old days
Moved earth and heaven, that which we are, we are;
One equal temper of heroic hearts,
Made weak by time and fate, but strong in will
To strive, to seek, to find, and not to yield.

from The Palace of Art (1832, rev. 1842)

I built my soul a lordly pleasure-house,
    Wherein at ease for aye to dwell.
I said, "O Soul, make merry and carouse,
    Dear soul, for all is well."

A huge crag-platform, smooth as burnish'd brass,
    I chose. The ranged ramparts bright
From level meadow-bases of deep grass
    Suddenly scaled the light.

Thereon I built it firm. Of ledge or shelf
    The rock rose clear, or winding stair.

My soul would live alone unto herself
    In her high palace there.

And "while the world runs round and round," I said,
    "Reign thou apart, a quiet king,
Still as, while Saturn whirls his stedfast shade
    Sleeps on his luminous ring."

To which my soul made answer readily:
    "Trust me, in bliss I shall abide
In this great mansion, that is built for me,
    So royal-rich and wide."

              * * * * * * * * * * * *
              * * * * * * * * * * * *⁵

Four courts I made, East, West and South and North,
    In each a squared lawn, wherefrom
The golden gorge of dragons spouted forth
    A flood of fountain-foam.

And round the cool green courts there ran a row
    Of cloisters, branch'd like mighty woods,
Echoing all night to that sonorous flow
    Of spouted fountain-floods.

And round the roofs a gilded gallery
    That lent broad verge to distant lands,
Far as the wild swan wings, to where the sky
    Dipt down to sea and sands.

From those four jets four currents in one swell
    Across the mountain stream'd below
In misty folds, that floating as they fell
    Lit up a torrent-bow.

And high on every peak a statue seem'd
    To hang on tiptoe, tossing up

---

⁵ This double row of stars reproduces the original format of the published poem.

A cloud of incense of all odour steam'd
 From out a golden cup.

So that she thought, "And who shall gaze upon
 My palace with unblinded eyes,
While this great bow will waver in the sun,
 And that sweet incense rise?"

For that sweet incense rose and never fail'd,
 And, while day sank or mounted higher,
The light aerial gallery, golden-rail'd,
 Burnt like a fringe of fire.

Likewise the deep-set windows, stain'd and traced,
 Would seem slow-flaming crimson fires
From shadow'd grots of arches interlaced,
 And tipt with frost-like spires.

* * * * * * * * * * * *
* * * * * * * * * * * *

Break, Break, Break (1842)

Break, break, break,
On thy cold gray stones, O Sea!
And I would that my tongue could utter
The thoughts that arise in me.

O well for the fisherman's boy,
That he shouts with his sister at play!
O well for the sailor lad,
That he sings in his boat on the bay!

And the stately ships go on
To their haven under the hill;
But O for the touch of a vanish'd hand,
And the sound of a voice that is still!

Break, break, break,
At the foot of thy crags, O Sea!
But the tender grace of a day that is dead
Will never come back to me.

L'Envoi,[6] *from* The Day-Dream[7] *(1843)*

I.

You shake your head. A random string
Your finer female sense offends.
Well were it not a pleasant thing
To fall asleep with all one's friends;
To pass with all our social ties
To silence from the paths of men;
And every hundred years to rise
And learn the world, and sleep again;
To sleep thro' terms of mighty wars,
And wake on science grown to more,
On secrets of the brain, the stars,
As wild as aught of fairy lore;
And all that else the years will show,
The Poet-forms of stronger hours,
The vast Republics that may grow,
The Federations and the Powers;
Titanic forces taking birth
In divers seasons, divers climes;
For we are Ancients of the earth,
And in the morning of the times.

II.

So sleeping, so aroused from sleep

---

[6] L'Envoi is a closing thought attached to a poem or literary work, usually conveying a
moral or addressing the poem to a particular person.

[7] "The Day Dream" is an expanded version of "The Sleeping Beauty," which Tennyson
wrote in 1830, shortly after the death of Arthur Hallam.

Thro' sunny decads new and strange,
Or gay quinquenniads would we reap
The flower and quintessence of change.

III.

Ah, yet would I and would I might!
So much your eyes my fancy take
Be still the first to leap to light
That I might kiss those eyes awake!
For, am I right or am I wrong,
To choose your own you did not care;
You'd have my moral from the song,
And I will take my pleasure there:
And, am I right or am I wrong,
My fancy, ranging thro' and thro',
To search a meaning for the song,
Perforce will still revert to you;
Nor finds a closer truth than this
All-graceful head, so richly curl'd,
And evermore a costly kiss
The prelude to some brighter world.

IV.

For since the time when Adam first
Embraced his Eve in happy hour,
And every bird of Eden burst
In carol, every bud to flower,
What eyes, like thine, have waken'd hopes?
What lips, like thine, so sweetly join'd?
Where on the double rosebud droops
The fullness of the pensive mind;
Which all too dearly self-involved,
Yet sleeps a dreamless sleep to me;
A sleep by kisses undissolved,
That lets thee neither hear nor see:
But break it. In the name of wife,

And in the rights that name may give,
Are clasp'd the moral of thy life,
And that for which I care to live.

Sweet and Low, from The Princess (1847)

Sweet and low, sweet and low
Wind of the western sea,
Low, low, breathe and blow,
Wind of the western sea!
Over the rolling waters go,
Come from the dying moon, and blow,
Blow him again to me,
While my little one, while my pretty one, sleeps.

Sleep and rest, sleep and rest,
Father will come to thee soon;
Rest, rest, on mother's breast,
Father will come to thee soon;
Father will come to his babe in the nest,
Silver sails all out of the west
Under the silver moon!
Sleep my little one, sleep my pretty one, sleep.

Ring Out, Wild Bells, from In Memoriam[8] (1850)

Ring out, wild bells, to the wild sky,
The flying cloud, the frosty light:
The year is dying in the night;
Ring out, wild bells, and let him die.

Ring out the old, ring in the new,
Ring, happy bells, across the snow:

---

[8] "In Memoriam" was written in honor of the poet's beloved friend, Arthur Hallam. Hallam died at the age of 22, shortly before he was to be married to Tennyson's sister.

The year is going, let him go;
Ring out the false, ring in the true.

Ring out the grief that saps the mind,
For those that here we see no more;
Ring out the feud of rich and poor,
Ring in redress to all mankind.

Ring out a slowly dying cause,
And ancient forms of party strife;
Ring in the nobler modes of life,
With sweeter manners, purer laws.

Ring out the want, the care, the sin,
The faithless coldness of the times;
Ring out, ring out my mournful rhymes,
But ring the fuller minstrel in.

Ring out false pride in place and blood,
The civic slander and the spite;
Ring in the love of truth and right,
Ring in the common love of good.

Ring out old shapes of foul disease;
Ring out the narrowing lust of gold;
Ring out the thousand wars of old,
Ring in the thousand years of peace.

Ring in the valiant man and free,
The larger heart, the kindlier hand;
Ring out the darkness of the land,
Ring in the Christ that is to be.

The Eagle (1851)

He clasps the crag with crooked hands;
Close to the sun in lonely lands,
Ring'd with the azure world, he stands.

The wrinkled sea beneath him crawls;
He watches from his mountain walls,
And like a thunderbolt he falls.

The Charge of the Light Brigade[9] *(1854)*

I.

Half a league, half a league,
Half a league onward,
All in the valley of Death
Rode the six hundred.
'Forward, the Light Brigade!'
'Charge for the guns!' he said:
Into the valley of Death
Rode the six hundred.

II.

'Forward, the Light Brigade!'
Was there a man dismay'd?
Not tho' the soldier knew
Some one had blunder'd:
Their's not to make reply,
Their's not to reason why,
Their's but to do and die:
Into the valley of Death
Rode the six hundred.

III.

Cannon to right of them,
Cannon to left of them,
Cannon in front of them

---

[9] In 1854, *The Charge of the Light Brigade* was published in *The Examiner*. The setting is the Battle of Balaclava during the Crimean War. In this battle, British cavalry (the Light Brigade) charged down a narrow valley lined on three sides with Russian troops. This hopeless attack, from which only one-third of the cavalry returned, was the result of a miscommunication of orders from the British commander. Tennyson's poem celebrates and immortalizes the bravery and loyalty of the soldiers in the Light Brigade.

Volley'd and thunder'd;
Storm'd at with shot and shell,
Boldly they rode and well,
Into the jaws of Death,
Into the mouth of Hell
Rode the six hundred.

IV.

Flash'd all their sabres bare,
Flash'd as they turn'd in air,
Sabring the gunners there,
Charging an army, while
All the world wonder'd:
Plunged in the battery-smoke
Right thro' the line they broke;
Cossack and Russian
Reel'd from the sabre-stroke
Shatter'd and sunder'd.
Then they rode back, but not
Not the six hundred.

V.

Cannon to right of them,
Cannon to left of them,
Cannon behind them
Volley'd and thunder'd;
Storm'd at with shot and shell,
While horse and hero fell,
They that had fought so well
Came thro' the jaws of Death,
Back from the mouth of Hell,
All that was left of them,
Left of six hundred.

VI.

When can their glory fade?
O the wild charge they made!
All the world wondered.
Honor the charge they made!
Honor the Light Brigade,
Noble six hundred!

The Brook (1864)

I come from haunts of coot and hern,
I make a sudden sally
And sparkle out among the fern,
To bicker down a valley.

By thirty hills I hurry down,
Or slip between the ridges,
By twenty thorpes, a little town,
And half a hundred bridges.

Till last by Philip's farm I flow
To join the brimming river,
For men may come and men may go,
But I go on for ever.

I chatter over stony ways,
In little sharps and trebles,
I bubble into eddying bays,
I babble on the pebbles.

With many a curve my banks I fret
By many a field and fallow,
And many a fairy foreland set
With willow-weed and mallow.

I chatter, chatter, as I flow
To join the brimming river,

For men may come and men may go,
But I go on for ever.

I wind about, and in and out,
With here a blossom sailing,
And here and there a lusty trout,
And here and there a grayling,

And here and there a foamy flake
Upon me, as I travel
With many a silvery waterbreak
Above the golden gravel,

And draw them all along, and flow
To join the brimming river
For men may come and men may go,
But I go on for ever.

I steal by lawns and grassy plots,
I slide by hazel covers;
I move the sweet forget-me-nots
That grow for happy lovers.

I slip, I slide, I gloom, I glance,
Among my skimming swallows;
I make the netted sunbeam dance
Against my sandy shallows.

I murmur under moon and stars
In brambly wildernesses;
I linger by my shingly bars;
I loiter round my cresses;

And out again I curve and flow
To join the brimming river,
For men may come and men may go,
But I go on for ever.

ALFRED, LORD TENNYSON

from *The Passing of Arthur in Idylls of the King*[10] *(1869)*

And answer made King Arthur, breathing hard:
'My end draws nigh; 'tis time that I were gone.
Make broad thy shoulders to receive my weight,
And bear me to the margin; yet I fear
My wound hath taken cold, and I shall die.'

So saying, from the pavement he half rose,
Slowly, with pain, reclining on his arm,
And looking wistfully with wide blue eyes
As in a picture. Him Sir Bedivere
Remorsefully regarded through his tears,
And would have spoken, but he found not words;
Then took with care, and kneeling on one knee,
O'er both his shoulders drew the languid hands,
And rising bore him through the place of tombs.

But, as he walked, King Arthur panted hard,
Like one that feels a nightmare on his bed
When all the house is mute. So sighed the King,
Muttering and murmuring at his ear, 'Quick, quick!
I fear it is too late, and I shall die.'

But the other swiftly strode from ridge to ridge,
Clothed with his breath, and looking, as he walked,
Larger than human on the frozen hills.
He heard the deep behind him, and a cry
Before. His own thought drove him like a goad.
Dry clashed his harness in the icy caves
And barren chasms, and all to left and right
The bare black cliff clanged round him, as he based
His feet on juts of slippery crag that rang
Sharp-smitten with the dint of armed heels—

---

[10] The *Idylls of the King* is a series of poems in which Tennyson sets forth his vision of the
Arthurian legends. Much of his inspiration comes from *Le Morte d'Arthur,* by Thomas
Malory.

And on a sudden, lo! the level lake,
And the long glories of the winter moon.

Then saw they how there hove a dusky barge,
Dark as a funeral scarf from stem to stern,
Beneath them; and descending they were ware
That all the decks were dense with stately forms,
Black-stoled, black-hooded, like a dream—by these
Three Queens with crowns of gold: and from them rose
A cry that shivered to the tingling stars,
And, as it were one voice, an agony
Of lamentation, like a wind that shrills
All night in a waste land, where no one comes,
Or hath come, since the making of the world.

Then murmured Arthur, 'Place me in the barge.'
So to the barge they came. There those three Queens
Put forth their hands, and took the King, and wept.
But she, that rose the tallest of them all
And fairest, laid his head upon her lap,
And loosed the shattered casque, and chafed his hands,
And called him by his name, complaining loud,
And dropping bitter tears against a brow
Striped with dark blood: for all his face was white
And colourless, and like the withered moon
Smote by the fresh beam of the springing east;
And all his greaves and cuisses dashed with drops
Of onset; and the light and lustrous curls—
That made his forehead like a rising sun
High from the dais-throne—were parched with dust;
Or, clotted into points and hanging loose,
Mixed with the knightly growth that fringed his lips.
So like a shattered column lay the King;
Not like that Arthur who, with lance in rest,
From spur to plume a star of tournament,
Shot through the lists at Camelot, and charged

Before the eyes of ladies and of kings.

Then loudly cried the bold Sir Bedivere:
'Ah! my Lord Arthur, whither shall I go?
Where shall I hide my forehead and my eyes?
For now I see the true old times are dead,
When every morning brought a noble chance,
And every chance brought out a noble knight.
Such times have been not since the light that led
The holy Elders with the gift of myrrh.
But now the whole Round Table is dissolved
Which was an image of the mighty world,
And I, the last, go forth companionless,
And the days darken round me, and the years,
Among new men, strange faces, other minds.'

And slowly answered Arthur from the barge:
'The old order changeth, yielding place to new,
And God fulfils himself in many ways,
Lest one good custom should corrupt the world.
Comfort thyself: what comfort is in me?
I have lived my life, and that which I have done
May He within himself make pure! but thou,
If thou shouldst never see my face again,
Pray for my soul. More things are wrought by prayer
Than this world dreams of. Wherefore, let thy voice
Rise like a fountain for me night and day.
For what are men better than sheep or goats
That nourish a blind life within the brain,
If, knowing God, they lift not hands of prayer
Both for themselves and those who call them friend?
For so the whole round earth is every way
Bound by gold chains about the feet of God.
But now farewell. I am going a long way
With these thou seest—if indeed I go
(For all my mind is clouded with a doubt)—
To the island-valley of Avilion;

Where falls not hail, or rain, or any snow,
Nor ever wind blows loudly; but it lies
Deep-meadowed, happy, fair with orchard lawns
And bowery hollows crowned with summer sea,
Where I will heal me of my grievous wound.'

So said he, and the barge with oar and sail
Moved from the brink, like some full-breasted swan
That, fluting a wild carol ere her death,
Ruffles her pure cold plume, and takes the flood
With swarthy webs. Long stood Sir Bedivere
Revolving many memories, till the hull
Looked one black dot against the verge of dawn,
And on the mere the wailing died away.

To Virgil, Written at the Request of the Mantuana for the XIX
Centenary of Virgil's Death (1881)

Roman Virgil, thou that singest
    Ilion's lofty temples robed in fire,
Ilion falling, Rome arising,
    wars, and filial faith, and Dido's pyre;

Landscape-lover, lord of language
    more than he that sang the Works and Days,
All the chosen coin of fancy
    flashing out from many a golden phrase;

Thou that singest wheat and woodland,
    tilth and vineyard, hive and horse and herd;
All the charm of all the Muses
    often flowering in a lonely word;

Poet of the happy Tityrus
    piping underneath his beechen bowers;
Poet of the poet-satyr
    whom the laughing shepherd bound with flowers;

51

ALFRED, LORD TENNYSON

Chanter of the Pollio, glorying
    in the blissful years again to be,
Summers of the snakeless meadow,
    unlaborious earth and oarless sea;

Thou that seest Universal
    Nature moved by Universal Mind;
Thou majestic in thy sadness
    at the doubtful doom of human kind;

Light among the vanished ages;
    star that gildest yet this phantom shore;
Golden branch amid the shadows,
    kings and realms that pass to rise no more;

Now thy Forum roars no longer,
    fallen every purple Cæsar's dome—
Tho' thine ocean-roll of rhythm
    sound for ever of Imperial Rome—

Now the Rome of slaves hath perished,
    and the Rome of freemen holds her place,
I, from out the Northern Island
    sunder'd once from all the human race,

I salute thee, Montovano,
    I that loved thee since my day began,
Wielder of the stateliest measure
    ever moulded by the lips of man.

Milton

O mighty-mouth'd inventor of harmonies,
O skill'd to sing of Time or Eternity,
    God-gifted organ-voice of England,
        Milton, a name to resound for ages;
Whose Titan angels, Gabriel, Abdiel,

Starr'd from Jehovah's gorgeous armouries,
  Tower, as the deep-domed empyrean
    Rings to the roar of an angel onset—
Me rather all that bowery loneliness,
The brooks of Eden mazily murmuring,
  And bloom profuse and cedar arches
    Charm, as a wanderer out in ocean,
Where some refulgent sunset of India
Streams o'er a rich ambrosial ocean isle,
  And crimson-hued the stately palm-woods
    Whisper in odorous heights of even.

Frater Ave Atque Vale[11] *(1883)*

Row us out from Desenzano, to your Sirmione row!
So they row'd, and there we landed–'O venusta Sirmio!'
There to me thro' all the groves of olive in the summer glow,
There beneath the Roman ruin where the purple flowers grow,
Came that 'Ave atque Vale' of the Poet's hopeless woe,
Tenderest of Roman poets nineteen-hundred years ago,
'Frater Ave atque Vale'–as we wander'd to and fro
Gazing at the Lydian laughter of the Garda Lake below
Sweet Catullus's all-but-island, olive-silvery Sirmio!

Crossing the Bar[12] *(1889)*

Sunset and evening star,
And one clear call for me!
And may there be no moaning of the bar,
When I put out to sea,

But such a tide as moving seems asleep,
Too full for sound and foam,

---

[11] Frater, Ave, Atque Vale *Hail, brother, and also farewell.* Tennyson is alluding to a poem of the late Roman Republic by Catullus.

[12] "Crossing the Bar" is, by tradition, the last poem in an anthology of Tennyson's works.

When that which drew from out the boundless deep
  Turns again home.

Twilight and evening bell,
And after that the dark!
And may there be no sadness of farewell,
When I embark;

For tho' from out our bourne of Time and Place
The flood may bear me far,
I hope to see my Pilot face to face
When I have crost the bar.

George Herbert

O f all our religious poets, of this time (the seventeenth century) at least, George Herbert is the greatest. He was born in 1593 near the town of Montgomery, and was the son of a noble family, but his father died when he was little more than three, leaving his mother to bring up George with his nine brothers and sisters.

George Herbert's mother was a good and beautiful woman, and she loved her children so well that the poet said afterwards she had been twice a mother to him.

At twelve he was sent to Westminster school where we are told "the beauties of his pretty behaviour shined" so that he seemed "to become the care of Heaven and of a particular good angel to guard and guide him."[1]

At fifteen he went to Trinity College, Cambridge. And now, although separated from his "dear and careful Mother" he did not forget her or all that she had taught him. Already he was a poet. We find him sending verses as a New Year gift to his mother and writing to her that "my poor abilities in

---

[1] Izaak Walton, *The Life of Mr. George Herbert,* (London: Macmillan, 1906)

poetry shall be all and ever consecrated to God's glory."[2]

As the years went on Herbert worked hard and became a gently good, as well as a learned man, and in time he was given the post of Public Orator at the University. This post brought him into touch with the court and with the King. Of this George Herbert was glad, for although he was a good and saintly man, he longed to be a courtier. Often now he went to court hoping for some great post. But James I died in 1625 and with him died George Herbert's hope of rising to be great in the world.

For a time, then, he left court and went into the country, and there he passed through a great struggle with himself. The question he had to settle was "whether he should return to the painted pleasure of a court life" or become a priest.

In the end he decided to become a priest, and when a friend tried to dissuade him from the calling as one too much below his birth, he answered: "It hath been judged formerly, that the domestic servants of the King of Heaven should be one of the noblest families on earth. And though the iniquity of late times have made clergymen meanly valued, and the sacred name of priest contemptible, yet I will labor to make it honorable. . . . And I will labor to be like my Saviour, by making humility lovely in the eyes of all men, and by following the merciful and meek example of my dear Jesus."

But before Herbert was fully ordained a great change came into his life. The Church of England was now Protestant and

---

[2] Walton, *op. cit.*

priests were allowed to marry, and George Herbert married. The story of how he met his wife is pretty.

Herbert was such a cheerful and good man that he had many friends. It was said, indeed, that he had no enemy. Among his many friends was one named Danvers, who loved him so much that he said nothing would make him so happy as that George should marry one of his nine daughters. But specially he wished him to marry his daughter Jane, for he loved her best, and would think of no more happy fate for her than to be the wife of such a man as George Herbert. He talked of George so much to Jane that she loved him without having seen him. George too heard of Jane and wished to meet her. And at last after a long time they met. Each had heard so much about the other that they seemed to know one another already, and like the prince and princess in a fairy tale, they loved at once, and three days later they were married.

Soon after this, George Herbert was offered the living of Bemerton near Salisbury. But although he had already made up his mind to become a priest he was as yet only a deacon. This sudden offer made him fearful. He began again to question himself and wonder if he was good enough for such a high calling. For a month he fasted and prayed over it. But in the end Laud, Bishop of London, assured him "that the refusal of it was a sin." So Herbert put off his sword and gay silken clothes, and putting on the long dark robe of a priest turned his back for ever to thoughts of a court life. "I now look back upon my aspiring thoughts," he said, "and think myself more happy than if I had attained what I so ambitiously thirsted for. I can now behold the court with an impartial eye, and see plainly that it is made up of fraud and titles and flattery, and many other such empty, imaginary, painted pleasures." And having turned his back on all gayety, he began the life which earned for him the name of "saintly George Herbert." He taught his people, preached to them, and prayed with them so lovingly that they loved him in return. "Some of the meaner sort of his parish did so love and reverence Mr. Herbert that they would let their plough rest when Mr. Herbert's saint's bell rang to prayers, that they might also offer their devotions to God with him; and would then return back to their plough. And his most holy life was such, that it begot such reverence to God and to him, that they thought themselves the happier when they carried Mr. Herbert's blessing back with them to their labour."

. . . besides being a parson Herbert was a courtier and a fine gentleman. His courtly friends were surprised that he should lower himself by helping a poor man with his own hands. But that is just one thing that we have to remember about Herbert, he had nothing of the puritan in him, he was a cavalier, a courtier, yet he showed the world that it was possible to be these and still be a good man. He did not believe that any honest work was a "dirty employment.

. . . His life, one would think, was busy enough, and full enough, yet amid it all he found time to write. Besides many poems he wrote for his own guidance a book called *The*

Country Parson. It is a book, says Walton, "so full of plain, prudent, and useful rules that that country parson that can spare 12d. and yet wants it is scarce excusable."

But Herbert's happy, useful days at Bemerton were all too short. In 1632, before he had held his living three years, he died, and was buried by his sorrowing people beneath the altar of his own little church.—Henrietta E. Marshall, *English Literature for Boys and Girls*

George Herbert's poems were not published until after his death. Another biographer writes of Herbert's poetry:

"O day most calm, most bright," sang George Herbert, and we may safely take that single line as expressive of the whole spirit of his writings. Professor Palmer, whose scholarly edition of this poet's works is a model for critics and editors, calls Herbert the first in English poetry who spoke face to face with God. That may be true; but it is interesting to note that not a poet of the first half of the seventeenth century, not even the gayest of the Cavaliers, but has written some noble verse of prayer or aspiration, which expresses the underlying Puritan spirit of his age. Herbert is the greatest, the most consistent of them all. In all the others the Puritan struggles against the Cavalier, or the Cavalier breaks loose from the restraining Puritan; but in Herbert the struggle is past and peace has come. That his life was not all calm, that the Puritan in him had struggled desperately before it subdued the pride and idleness of the Cavalier, is evident to one who reads between his lines:

> I struck the board and cry'd, No more!
>> I will abroad.
> What? Shall I ever sigh and pine?
> My lines and life are free, free as the road,
>> Loose as the wind.

There speaks the Cavalier of the university and the court; and as one reads to the end of the little poem, which he calls by the suggestive name of "The Collar," he may know that he is reading condensed biography.

. . . Just before his death he gave some manuscripts to a friend, and his message is worthy of John Bunyan:

"Deliver this little book to my dear brother Ferrar, and tell him he shall find in it a picture of the many spiritual conflicts that have passed betwixt God and my soul before I could subject mine to the will of Jesus my master, in whose service I have now found perfect freedom. Desire him to read it; and then, if he can think it may turn to the advantage of any dejected poor soul, let it be made public; if not, let him burn it, for I and it are less than the least of God's mercies."—William J. Long, *English Literature, Its History and Its Significance for the English-Speaking World*

Students who have already met C. S. Lewis will be interested to know the effect of Herbert's poetry on the unbelieving English professor:

"But the most alarming was George Herbert. Here was a man who seemed to me to excel all the authors I had read in

conveying the very quality of life as we live it from moment
to moment, but the wretched fellow, instead of doing it
all directly, insisted on mediating it through what I still
would have called the "Christian mythology."—C. S. Lewis,
Surprised By Joy

He describes the influence of authors past and present, pagan and
Christian, as that of hounds chasing a fox:

> . . . bedraggled and weary, hounds barely a field behind.
> And now nearly everyone (one way or another) was in the
> pack: Plato, Dante, MacDonald, Herbert, Barfield, Tolkien,
> Dyson, Joy itself. Everyone and everything had joined the
> other side."—C. S. Lewis, *Surprised By Joy*

GEORGE HERBERT

Redemption (1633)

Having been tenant long to a rich Lord,
      Not thriving, I resolved to be bold,
      And make a suit unto him, to afford
A new small-rented lease, and cancell th' old.

In heaven at his manour I him sought:
      They told me there, that he was lately gone
      About some land, which he had dearly bought
Long since on earth, to take possession.

I straight return'd, and knowing his great birth,
      Sought him accordingly in great resorts ;
      In cities, theatres, gardens, parks, and courts:
At length I heard a ragged noise and mirth

      Of theeves and murderers: there I him espied,
      Who straight, Your suit is granted, said, and died.

Sinne I (1633)

LORD, with what care hast thou begirt us round !
      Parents first season us: then schoolmasters
      Deliver us to laws ; They send us bound
To rules of reason, holy messengers,

Pulpits and sundayes, sorrow dogging sinne,
      Afflictions sorted, anguish of all sizes,
      Fine nets and stratagems to catch us in,
Bibles laid open, millions of surprises,

Blessings beforehand, tyes of gratefulnesse,
      The sound of glorie ringing in our eares ;
      Without, our shame ; within, our consciences ;
Angels and grace, eternall hopes and fears.

Yet all these fences and their whole aray
One cunning bosome-sinne blows quite away.

Easter Wings (1633)

LORD, who createdst man in wealth and store,
   Though foolishly he lost the same,
     Decaying more and more,
       Till he became
        Most poor:

        With thee
       O let me rise
     As larks, harmoniously,
   And sing this day thy victories:
Then shall the fall further the flight in me.

My tender age in sorrow did beginne:
   And still with sicknesses and shame
     Thou didst so punish sinne,
       That I became
        Most thinne.

        With thee
      Let me combine,
    And feel this day thy victorie,
  For, if I imp my wing on thine,
Affliction shall advance the flight in me.

The Elixir (1633)

     Teach me, my God and King,
     In all things Thee to see,
  And what I do in anything,
      To do it as for Thee.

Not rudely, as a beast,
　　To run into action;
But still to make Thee prepossest,
　　And give it his perfection.

A man that looks on glass,
　　On it may stay his eye,
Or, if he pleaseth, through it pass,
　　And then the heav'n espy.

All may of Thee partake ;
　　Nothing can be so mean
Which with his tincture (for Thy sake)
　　Will not grow bright and clean.

A servant with this clause
　　Makes drudgery divine:
Who sweeps a room as for Thy laws,
　　Makes that and th' action fine.

This is the famous stone
　　That turneth all to gold ;
For that which God doth touch and own
　　Cannot for less be told.

The Pilgrimage (1633)

I Travell'd on, seeing the hill, where lay
　　　　　My expectation.
　　A long it was and weary way.
　　The gloomy cave of Desperation
I left on th' one, and on the other side
　　　　　The rock of Pride.

And so I came to phancies medow strow'd
                With many a flower:
      Fain would I here have made abode,
      But I was quicken'd by my houre.
So to cares cops[3] I came, and there got through
                With much ado.

That led me to the wilde of Passion, which
                Some call the wold;
      A wasted place, but sometimes rich.
      Here I was robb'd of all my gold,
Save one good Angell,which a friend had ti'd
                Close to my side.

At length I got unto the gladsome hill,[4]
                Where lay my hope,
      Where lay my heart; and climbing still,
      When I had gain'd the brow and top,
A lake of brackish waters on the ground
                Was all I found.

With that abash'd and struck with many a sting
                Of swarming fears,
      I fell, and cry'd, Alas my King!
      Can both the way and end be tears?
Yet taking heart I rose, and then perceiv'd
                I was deceiv'd:

My hill was further: so I flung away,
                Yet heard a crie

---

[3] cops *copse (a small thicket or grove of trees)*

[4] ... "remembering the wide influence of Herbert's poetry, it is an interesting question whether Bunyan received the idea of his immortal work from this Pilgrimage.—William J. Long, *English Literature, Its History and Its Significance for the English-Speaking World*

GEORGE HERBERT

Just as I went, None goes that way
And lives: If that be all, said I,
After so foul a journey death is fair,
And but a chair.

Prayer I (1633)

Prayer the Churches banquet, Angels age,
Gods breath in man returning to his birth,
The soul in paraphrase, heart in pilgrimage,
The Christian plummet sounding heav'n and earth;

Engine against th' Almightie, sinner's towre,
Reversed thunder, Christ-side-piercing spear,
The six daies world-transposing in an houre,
A kinde of tune, which all things heare and fear;

Softnesse, and peace, and joy, and love, and blisse,
Exalted Manna, gladnesse of the best,
Heaven in ordinarie, man well drest,
The milkie way, the bird of Paradise,

Church-bels beyond the stars heard, the souls bloud,
The land of spices, something understood.

Vertue (1633)

Sweet day, so cool, so calm, so bright,
The bridall of the earth and skie:
The dew shall weep thy fall to-night ;
For thou must die.

Sweet rose, whose hue angrie and brave
Bids the rash gazer wipe his eye,
Thy root is ever in its grave,
And thou must die.

Sweet spring, full of sweet dayes and roses,
A box where sweets compacted lie,
My musick shows ye have your closes,
                    And all must die.

Onely a sweet and vertuous soul,
Like season'd timber, never gives ;
But though the whole world turn to coal,
                    Then chiefly lives.

The Collar (1633)

I struck the board, and cry'd, No more ;
                    I will abroad.
    What? shall I ever sigh and pine?
My lines and life are free; free as the rode,
    Loose as the winde, as large as store.
                    Shall I be still in suit?
    Have I no harvest but a thorn
    To let me bloud, and not restore
What I have lost with cordiall fruit?
                    Sure there was wine,
    Before my sighs did drie it: there was corn
            Before my tears did drown it.
    Is the yeare onely lost to me?
            Have I no bayes to crown it?
No flowers, no garlands gay? all blasted?
                    All wasted?
    Not so, my heart: but there is fruit,
            And thou hast hands.
    Recover all thy sigh-blown age
On double pleasures: leave thy cold dispute
Of what is fit, and not forsake thy cage,
                    Thy rope of sands,
Which pettie thoughts have made, and made to thee
    Good cable, to enforce and draw,

And be thy law,
While thou didst wink and wouldst not see.
Away; take heed:
I will abroad.
Call in thy deaths head there: tie up thy fears.
He that forbears
To suit and serve his need,
Deserves his load.
But as I rav'd and grew more fierce and wilde,
At every word,
Methought I heard one calling, *Childe*:
And I reply'd, *My Lord*.

Artillery (1633)

As I one evening sat before my cell,
Methought a star did shoot into my lap.
I rose and shook my clothes, as knowing well
That from small fires comes oft no small mishap;
When suddenly I heard one say,
"Do as thou usest, disobey,
Expel good motions from thy breast,
Which have the face of fire, but end in rest."

I, who had heard of music in the spheres,
But not of speech in stars, began to muse;
But turning to my God, whose ministers
The stars and all things are: "If I refuse,
Dread Lord," said I, "so oft my good,
Then I refuse not ev'n with blood
To wash away my stubborn thought;
For I will do or suffer what I ought.

"But I have also stars and shooters too,
Born where thy servants both artilleries use.

My tears and prayers night and day do woo
And work up to thee; yet thou dost refuse.
 Not but I am (I must say still)
 Much more obliged to do thy will
 Than thou to grant mine; but because
Thy promise now hath ev'n set thee thy laws.

"Then we are shooters both, and thou dost deign
To enter combat with us, and contest
With thine own clay. But I would parley fain:
Shun not my arrows, and behold my breast.
 Yet if thou shunnest, I am thine:
 I must be so, if I am mine.
 There is no articling with thee:
I am but finite, yet thine infinitely."

The Pulley (1633)

When God at first made man,
Having a glasse of blessings standing by ;
Let us (said he) poure on him all we can:
Let the worlds riches, which dispersed lie,
  Contract into a span.

  So strength first made a way ;
Then beautie flow'd, then wisdome, honour, pleasure:
When almost all was out, God made a stay,
Perceiving that alone, of all his treasure,
  Rest in the bottome lay.

  For if I should (said he)
Bestow this jewell also on my creature,
He would adore my gifts in stead of me,
And rest in Nature, not the God of Nature:
  So both should losers be.

Yet let him keep the rest,
But keep them with repining restlesnesse:
Let him be rich and wearie, that at least,
If goodnesse leade him not, yet wearinesse
　　May tosse him to my breast.

Aaron (1633)

Holiness on the head,
Light and perfection on the breast,
Harmonious bells below raising the dead
To lead them unto life and rest.
　　Thus are true Aarons drest.[5]

Profaneness in my head,
Defects and darkness in my breast,
A noise of passions ringing me for dead
Unto a place where is no rest:
　　Poor priest ! thus am I drest.

Only another head
I have another heart and breast,
Another music, making live, not dead,
Without whom I could have no rest:
　　In Him I am well drest.

Christ is my only head,
My alone only heart and breast,
My only music, striking me e'en dead ;
That to the old man I may rest,
　　And be in Him new drest.

So holy in my Head,
Perfect and light in my dear Breast,
My doctrine tuned by Christ (who is not dead,
But lives in me while I do rest),
　　Come, people; Aaron's drest.

[5] Exodus xxviii. 29-37

GEORGE HERBERT

Love III (1633)

Love bade me welcome, yet my soul drew back,
    Guilty of dust and sin.
But quick-ey'd Love, observing me grow slack
    From my first entrance in,
Drew nearer to me, sweetly questioning
    If I lack'd anything.

"A guest," I answer'd, "worthy to be here";
    Love said, "You shall be he."
"I, the unkind, the ungrateful? ah my dear,
    I cannot look on thee."
Love took my hand and smiling did reply,
    "Who made the eyes but I?"

"Truth, Lord, but I have marr'd them; let my shame
    Go where it doth deserve."
"And know you not," says Love, "who bore the blame?"
    "My dear, then I will serve."
"You must sit down," says Love, "and taste my meat."
    So I did sit and eat.

The Windows (1633)

LORD, how can man preach thy eternall word?
    He is a brittle crazie glasse:
Yet in thy temple thou dost him afford
    This glorious and transcendent place,
    To be a window, through thy grace.

But when thou dost anneal in glasse thy storie,
    Making thy life to shine within
The holy Preachers, then the light and glorie
    More rev'rend grows, and more doth win ;
    Which else shows watrish, bleak, and thin.

Doctrine and life, colours and light, in one
    When they combine and mingle, bring
A strong regard and aw: but speech alone
    Doth vanish like a flaring thing,
      And in the eare, not conscience ring.

The Agonie (1633)

Philosophers have measur'd mountains,
Fathom'd the depths of seas, of states, and kings,
Walk'd with a staffe to heav'n, and traced fountains:
    But there are two vast, spacious things,
The which to measure it doth more behove:
Yet few there are that sound them; Sinne and Love.

    Who would know Sinne, let him repair
Unto mount Olivet; there shall he see
A man so wrung with pains, that all his hair,
    His skinne, his garments bloudie be.
Sinne is that presse and vice, which forceth pain
To hunt his cruell food through ev'ry vein.

    Who knows not Love, let him assay
And taste that juice, which on the crosse a pike
Did set again abroach;1 then let him say
    If ever he did taste the like.
Love in that liquour sweet and most divine,
Which my God feels as bloud; but I, as wine.

Easter Song (1633)

I got me flowers to strew Thy way,
  I got me boughs off many a tree;
But Thou wast up by break of day,
  And brought'st Thy sweets along with Thee.

The sun arising in the East,
　Though he give light and th' East perfume,
If they should offer to contest
　With Thy arising, they presume.

　Can there be any day but this,
　Though many suns to shine endeavour?
We count three hundred, but we miss:
　There is but one, and that one ever.

Even-Song (1633)

Blest be the God of love,
Who gave me eyes, and light, and power this day,
　　Both to be busie, and to play.
　　But much more blest be God above,
　　　Who gave me sight alone,

　　Which to himself he did denie:
　　For when he sees my waies, I dy:
But I have got his sonne, and he hath none.

　　　What have I brought thee home
For this thy love? have I discharg'd the debt,
　　Which this dayes favour did beget?
　　I ranne ; but all I brought, was some.

　　　Thy diet, care, and cost
　　Do end in bubbles, balls of winde ;
　　Of winde to thee whom I have crost,
But balls of wilde-fire to my troubled minde.

　　　Yet still thou goest on,
And now with darknesse closest wearie eyes,
　　Saying to man, *It doth suffice:*
　　Henceforth repose; your work is done.

GEORGE HERBERT

Thus in thy Ebony box
Thou dost inclose us, till the day
Put our amendment in our way,
And give new wheels to our disorder'd clocks.

I muse, which shows more love,
The day or night ; that is the gale, this th' harbour ;
That is the walk, and this the arbour ;
Or that the garden, this the grove.

My God, thou art all love.
Not one poore minute 'scapes thy breast,
But brings a favour from above ;
And in this love, more than in bed, I rest.

WILLIAM SHAKESPEARE

Beyond Sir Hugh Clopton's noble old stone bridge that spans the Avon with fourteen splendid arches, rise the quaint gables and catehdral spire of Stratford town. In the days of good Queen Bess the houses were ancient plaster buildings crossed with timber and each had at the sides or rear a gay little garden, bright with flowers. In one of the best of those houses on Henley Street lived Master Will Shakespeare, a high spirited lad with a fine, courtly bearing and very pleasant eyes. His father, John Shakespeare, once High Bailiff, or Mayor, of Stratford, was a well-to-do merchant, a trader in hides, leather-goods, wool, meat, and goodness knows what besides. His mother, Mary Arden, was a blithe and womanly matron, who shed a warmth of tenderness through the merry little home circle.

Over in the old, old grammar school, with its jutting second story abutting on the street, Master Will and the other Stratford urchins learned their lessons. There they conned arithmetic, a bit of Latin and Greek, and the precepts of good manners from six o'clock in the morning till five-thirty in the evening, and the schoolmaster sitting over them was all too versed in the use of the birchen rod.—Olive Beaupré Miller, *My Book House: Halls of Fame*

William Shakespeare was baptised on the twenty-sixth day of April, in the Year of Our Lord 1564. As it was the custom to baptize babies shortly after birth, we can be reasonably sure that his birth was in close proximity to that date. Although we have little record of Shakespeare's early life, we do know much about the customs of the time and place in which he lived. It is very likely that

. . . once or twice at least he may have seen a play or pageant. His father went on prospering and was made chief bailiff of the town, and while in that office he entertained twice at least troups of strolling players, the Queen's Company and the Earl of Worcester's Company. It is very likely that little Will was taken to see the plays they acted. Then when he was eleven years old there was great excitement in the country town, for Queen Elizabeth came to visit the great Earl of Leicester at his castle of Kenilworth, not sixteen miles away. There were great doings then, and the Queen was received with all the magnificence and pomp that money could procure and imagination invent. Some of these grand shows Shakespeare must have seen.

Long afterwards he remembered perhaps how one evening he had stood among the crowd tiptoeing and eager to catch a glimpse of the great Queen as she sat enthroned on a golden chair. Her red- gold hair gleamed

and glittered with jewels under the flickering torchlight.
Around her stood a crowd of nobles and ladies only less
brilliant that she. Then, as William gazed and gazed, his
eyes aching with the dazzling lights, there was a movement
in the surging crowd, a murmur of "ohs" and "ahs." And,
turning, the boy saw another lady, another Queen, appear
from out the dark shadow of the trees. Stately and slowly
she moved across the grass. Then following her came a
winged boy with golden bow and arrows. This was the god
of Love, who roamed the world shooting his love arrows
at the hearts of men and women, making them love each
other. He aimed, he shot, the arrow flew, but the god
missed his aim and the lady passed on, beautiful, cold, free,
as before. Love could not touch her, he followed her but in
vain . . .—Henrietta Marshall, *English Literature for Boys
and Girls*

When he was eighteen, Will married Anne Hathaway, a farm girl
from a neighboring village, eight years his senior. Together they
had two daughters and one son. Only his daughters survived to
adulthood. Not much more is known about Shakespeare until
we see him again in the theatres of London around 1592, at age
twenty-eight.

We know very little of Shakespeare's life in London. As
an actor he never made a great name, never acted the chief
character in a play. But he acted sometimes in his own plays
and took the part, we are told, of a ghost in one, and of a
servant in another, neither of them great parts. He acted,
too, in plays written by other people. But it was as a writer

that he made a name, and that so quickly that others grew jealous of him. One called him "an upstart Crow, beautified in our feathers . . . in his own conceit the only Shake-scene in the country." But for the most part Shakespeare made friends even of rival authors, and many of them loved him well. He was good-tempered, merry, witty, and kindly, a most lovable man. "He was a handsome, well-shaped man, very good company, and a very ready and pleasant smooth wit," said one. "I loved the man and do honor to his memory, on this side of idolatry as much as any. He was indeed honest and of an open and free nature," said another. Others still called him a good fellow, gentle Shakespeare, sweet Master Shakespeare. I should like to think, too, that Spenser called him "our pleasant Willy."

. . . And so although outside his work we get only glimpses of the man, these glimpses taken together with his writings show us Will Shakespeare as a big-hearted man, a man who understood all and forgave all. He understood the little joys and sorrows that make up life. He understood the struggle to be good, and would not scorn people too greatly when they were bad. —Henrietta Marshall, *English Literature for Boys and Girls*

From 1592 to 1613, Shakespeare wrote plays and worked in the theatre, living mostly in London—except when the plague would break out in the city; then he would retire to Stratford. During this time, he also published a few narrative poems. His *Sonnets*—one hundred fify-four of them—were published in 1609, most likely the work of those many years as well.

Then as the years went on Shakespeare gave up all connection with London and the theater and settled down to a quiet country life. He planted trees, managed his estate, and showed that though he was the world's master-poet he was a good business man too. Everything prospered with him, his two daughters married well, and comfortably, and when not more than forty-three he held his first grandchild in his arms. It may be he looked forward to many happy peaceful years when death took him. He died of fever, brought on, no doubt, by the evil smells and bad air by which people lived surrounded in those days before they had learned to be clean in house and street.

Shakespeare was only fifty-two when he died. It was in the springtime of 1616 that he died, breathing his last upon

> "The uncertain glory of an April day
> Which now shows all the beauty of the sun
> And by and by a cloud takes all away."[1]

. . . It is from Shakespeare's works that we get the clearest picture of Elizabethan times. And yet, although we learn from him so much of what people did in those days, of how they talked and even of how they thought, the chief thing that we feel about Shakespeare's characters is, not that they are Elizabethan, but that they are human, that they are like ourselves, that they think, and say, and do, things which we ourselves might think, and say, and do.

There are many books we read which we think of

---

[1]   William Shakespeare, *Two Gentleman of Verona*

as very pretty, very quaint, very interesting—but old-
fashioned. But Shakespeare can never be old-fashioned,
because, although he is the outcome of his own times, and
gives us all the flavor of his own times, he gives us much
more. He understood human nature, he saw beneath the
outward dress, and painted for us real men and women.
And although fashion in dress and modes of living may
change, human nature does not change. "He was not of an
age but for all time," it was said of him about seven years
after his death, and now that nearly three hundred years
[*ed. note:* now more than 400 years] have come and gone
we still acknowledge the truth of those words.—Henrietta
Marshall, *English Literature for Boys and Girls*

Many scholars today think Shakespeare's literary achievements—
not to mention his knowledge of history and his apparent first-hand
knowledge of cities and countries far-removed from London would
have been completely beyond a man of William's education and
means. Theories abound about the "true identity" of Shakespeare,
most of them completely implausible, but a few which seem more
credible. Others debate theories of nature vs. nurture, as this
literary history of yesteryear reveals:

One who reads a few of Shakespeare's great plays and
then the meager story of his life is generally filled with a
vague wonder. Here is an unknown country boy, poor
and poorly educated according to the standards of his age,
who arrives at the great city of London and goes to work
at odd jobs in a theater. In a year or two he is associated
with scholars and dramatists, the masters of their age,

writing plays of kings and clowns, of gentlemen and heroes and noble women, all of whose lives he seems to know by intimate association. In a few years more he leads all that brilliant group of poets and dramatists who have given undying glory to the Age of Elizabeth. Play after play runs from his pen, mighty dramas of human life and character following one another so rapidly that good work seems impossible; yet they stand the test of time, and their poetry is still unrivaled in any language. For all this great work the author apparently cares little, since he makes no attempt to collect or preserve his writings. A thousand scholars have ever since been busy collecting, identifying, classifying the works which this magnificent workman tossed aside so carelessly when he abandoned the drama and retired to his native village. He has a marvelously imaginative and creative mind; but he invents few, if any, new plots or stories. He simply takes an old play or an old poem, makes it over quickly, and lo! this old familiar material glows with the deepest thoughts and the tenderest feelings that ennoble our humanity; and each new generation of men finds it more wonderful than the last. How did he do it? That is still an unanswered question and the source of our wonder.

There are, in general, two theories to account for Shakespeare. The romantic school of writers have always held that in him "all came from within"; that his genius was his sufficient guide; and that to the overmastering power of his genius alone we owe all his great works. Practical, unimaginative men, on the other hand, assert that in Shakespeare "all came from without," and that we must study his environment rather than his genius, if we are to understand him. He lived in a play-loving age; he studied the crowds, gave them what they wanted, and simply reflected their own thoughts and feelings. In reflecting the English crowd about him he unconsciously reflected all crowds, which are alike in all ages; hence his continued popularity. And in being guided by public sentiment he was not singular, but followed the plain path that every good dramatist has always followed to success.

Probably the truth of the matter is to be found somewhere between these two extremes. Of his great genius there can be no question; but there are other things to consider. As we have already noticed, Shakespeare was trained, like his fellow workmen, first as an actor, second as a reviser of old plays, and last as an independent dramatist. He worked with other playwrights and learned their secret. Like them, he studied and followed the public taste, and his work indicates at least three stages, from his first somewhat crude experiments to his finished masterpieces. So it would seem that in Shakespeare we have the result of hard work and of orderly human development, quite as much as of transcendent genius.

. . . Shakespeare holds, by general acclamation, the foremost place in the world's literature, and his overwhelming greatness renders it difficult to criticise or even to praise him. Two poets only, Homer and Dante, have been named with him; but each of these wrote within narrow limits, while Shakespeare's genius included all the world of nature and of men. In a word, he is the universal poet. To study nature in his works is like exploring a new and beautiful country; to study man in his works is like going into a great city, viewing the motley crowd as one views a great masquerade in which past and present mingle freely and familiarly, as if the dead were all living again. And the marvelous thing, in this masquerade of all sorts and conditions of men, is that Shakespeare lifts the mask from every face, lets us see the man as he is in his own soul, and shows us in each one some germ of good, some "soul of goodness" even in things evil. For Shakespeare strikes no uncertain note, and raises no doubts to add to the burden of your own. Good always overcomes evil in the long run; and love, faith, work, and duty are the four elements that in all ages make the world right. To criticise or praise the genius that creates these men and women is to criticise or praise humanity itself.

Of his influence in literature it is equally difficult to speak. Goethe expresses the common literary judgment when he says, "I do not remember that any book or person or event in my life ever made so great an impression upon me as the plays of Shakespeare." His influence upon our own language and thought is beyond calculation. Shakespeare and the King James Bible are the two great conservators of the English speech; and one who habitually reads them finds himself possessed of a style and vocabulary that are beyond criticism. Even those who read no Shakespeare are still unconsciously guided by him, for his thought and expression have so pervaded our life and literature that it is impossible, so long as one speaks the

English language, to escape his influence.

> His life was gentle, and the elements
> So mixed in him, that Nature might stand up
> And say to all the world, "This was a man!"[2]

---

[2]   William Shakespeare, *Julius Caesar*, V.v

WILLIAM SHAKESPEARE

Sonnet XVIII

Shall I compare thee to a summer's day?
Thou art more lovely and more temperate:
Rough winds do shake the darling buds of May,
And summer's lease hath all too short a date:
Sometime too hot the eye of heaven shines,
And often is his gold complexion dimm'd,
And every fair from fair sometime declines,
By chance, or nature's changing course untrimm'd:
But thy eternal summer shall not fade,
Nor lose possession of that fair thou ow'st,
Nor shall death brag thou wander'st in his shade,
When in eternal lines to time thou grow'st,
So long as men can breathe, or eyes can see,
So long lives this, and this gives life to thee.

Sonnet LV

Not marble or the gilded monuments
Of princes, shall outlive this powerful rhyme;
But you shall shine more bright in these contents
Than unswept stone, besmear'd with sluttish time.
When wasteful war shall statues overturn,
And broils root out the work of masonry,
Nor Mars his sword, nor war's quick fire shall burn
The living record of your memory.
'Gainst death, and all-oblivious enmity
Shall you pace forth; your praise shall still find room
Even in the eyes of all posterity
That wear this world out to the ending doom.
So, till the judgment that yourself arise,
You live in this, and dwell in lovers' eyes.

WILLIAM SHAKESPEARE

Lines from Hamlet, Act III, Scene 1

To be, or not to be- that is the question:
Whether 'tis nobler in the mind to suffer
The slings and arrows of outrageous fortune
Or to take arms against a sea of troubles,
And by opposing end them. To die- to sleep-
No more; and by a sleep to say we end
The heartache, and the thousand natural shocks
That flesh is heir to. 'Tis a consummation
Devoutly to be wish'd. To die- to sleep.
To sleep- perchance to dream: ay, there's the rub!
For in that sleep of death what dreams may come
When we have shuffled off this mortal coil,
Must give us pause. There's the respect
That makes calamity of so long life.
For who would bear the whips and scorns of time,
Th' oppressor's wrong, the proud man's contumely,
The pangs of despis'd love, the law's delay,
The insolence of office, and the spurns
That patient merit of th' unworthy takes,
When he himself might his quietus make
With a bare bodkin? Who would these fardels bear,
To grunt and sweat under a weary life,
But that the dread of something after death-
The undiscover'd country, from whose bourn
No traveller returns- puzzles the will,
And makes us rather bear those ills we have
Than fly to others that we know not of?
Thus conscience does make cowards of us all,
And thus the native hue of resolution
Is sicklied o'er with the pale cast of thought,
And enterprises of great pith and moment
With this regard their currents turn awry
And lose the name of action.